Negotiating with Backbone

Negotiating with Backbone

Eight Sales Strategies to Defend Your Price and Value

Reed K. Holden

Vice President, Publisher: Tim Moore
Associate Publisher and Director of Marketing: Amy Neidlinger
Executive Editor: Jeanne Glasser
Editorial Assistant: Pamela Boland
Operations Specialist: Jodi Kemper
Assistant Marketing Manager: Megan Graue
Cover Designer: Chuti Prasertsith
Managing Editor: Kristy Hart
Project Editor: Anne Goebel
Copy Editor: Paula Lowell
Proofreader: Christa White, Language Logistics
Indexer: Erika Millen
Compositor: Nonie Ratcliff
Manufacturing Buyer: Dan Uhrig

FT Press offers excellent discounts on this book when ordered in quantity for bulk purchases
or special sales. For more information, please contact U.S. Corporate and Government Sales,
1-800-382-3419, corpsales@pearsontechgroup.com. For sales outside the U.S., please contact
International Sales at international@pearson.com.

Printed in the United States of America
First Printing May 2012

ISBN-10: 0-13-306476-X
ISBN-13: 978-0-13-306476-6

Pearson Education LTD.
Pearson Education Australia PTY, Limited.
Pearson Education Singapore, Pte. Ltd.
Pearson Education Asia, Ltd.
Pearson Education Canada, Ltd.
Pearson Educación de Mexico, S.A. de C.V.
Pearson Education—Japan
Pearson Education Malaysia, Pte. Ltd.

Library of Congress Cataloging-in-Publication Data

Holden, Reed K.
  Negotiating with backbone : eight sales strategies to defend your price and value / Reed K.
Holden.
      p. cm.
  Includes index.
  ISBN 978-0-13-306476-6 (hardcover : alk. paper) -- ISBN 0-13-306476-X
  1. Selling. 2. Customer relations. 3. Negotiation. 4. Pricing. I. Title.
  HF5438.25.H638 2012
  658.8'101--dc23
                          2012007845

This book is dedicated to my children: Rebecca and Mark. You are successful individuals in your own ways with lots of backbone. You make a dad proud.

Contents

Acknowledgments

Books don't happen without the support of others. I'm grateful to a wide range of Holden Advisors people for their help as well as clients and friends over the years. All have provided insights and sometimes bruising input to help us craft this new model and the stories that support it.

Starting early in my career with research on buyer-seller relationships, Kevin Clancy of Copernicus, Randy Chapman of University of Michigan's Ross School of Business, and Tom Nagle of Monitor were the key influencing subject matter experts. The model evolved with further help from Tom Nagle and Dick Harmer while we were together growing Strategic Pricing Group and working on the second and third editions of *The Strategy and Tactics of Pricing*. A special thanks to Elaine Kelly who helped us start the first real business and took the brunt of the calls from procurement many years ago.

Later, when the team started Holden Advisors, I expanded the initial buyer behavior model to include the poker player, and Tom Sant of Hyde Park Partners was an early supporter and cheerleader. He helped put us on track, away from "dense prose," and initially floated the idea of a book on the subject. The model evolved to its current form with the support of a client in Australia. Many thanks to Neil Wilson, Jeanette Conrick, and Mark Johnson for their initial and continued support, and Andrew Jacka for becoming a strong supporter and collaborator as we evolved this model. Subsequent work in different geographic regions included people who were attentive and constructive, and while too many to mention—your help was appreciated.

Our internal team of consultants, led by Alison Yama with Alexander Beram, Jacqueline Davis, and Ellen Quackenbush, all worked tirelessly to shape up ideas into true training content for salespeople.

I owe a special thanks to the many procurement professionals over the years. For the sake of reputation, I won't name them,
but their stories and interactions helped build this model and refine
the tactics—and, of course—provided some of the stories. Special
thanks to procurement professional David Callaghan for his input and
perspective.

To help craft content and titles, I relied on a "kitchen cabinet" of
business colleagues. Their input made sure that the high points were
clear and that the title and artwork captured what we intended. A spe-
cial thanks for their efforts to Lewie Miller, Qvidian; Tom Sant, Hyde
Park Partners; Andrew Jacka, PricewaterhouseCoopers; Neil Wilson,
PricewaterhouseCoopers; Noel Capon, Columbia University; Wayne
Gartin, Novarum; Chris Hylen, Innovative Merchant Solutions; Mike
Lawson, Depuy Orthopedics; Adele McLean, icanCsolutions; Dino
Mele; Brent Melancon, Medtronic; Mike Mickelson, Medtronic;
Patrick McCullough, LifeCell; David Phillips; Pete Pichette, Span-
sion; Chris Provines, Holden Advisors; Andy Slusher, Golden Rev-
enue Solutions; Rebecca Holden, Heidrick & Struggles; Bob Knapp,
Neubrand; Vishal Kamar, Acme Alloys (India); and Paul Cutler.

Lewie Miller, CEO of Qvidian, took up this project with a very
special passion that I appreciated. He would chew over a question
until he had enough answers to find the solution. He provided many
great thoughts on the ultimate positioning for this book. And over
breakfast in his backyard one Sunday morning, he provided the story
of the "stomp" procurement person in the book.

I'm an idea guy and storyteller, not a great writer. This comes
with the correct word and turn of a phrase. One of two starting editors
of this project is John Kador. This is our second project together, and
things just keep getting better each time. This one started on a dime
and was a fun evolution of thoughts and words. John is a great editor
and has become a dear friend over the years.

Carolyn Holden was also an editor for this project. She is also
my business partner and wife. Think about that. Editors need to give

feedback, hard feedback. She was persistent and frank with her feedback and positioning. Yet we are still happily married, which tells you something about two things—the quality of her feedback and the quality of our relationship. She has truly been my number one fan.

This is our first time working with Pearson Education and we can't be more pleased with their professionalism and speed in getting this book to the market. Our Executive Editor is Jeanne Glasser, someone we have worked with over the years. We have learned to trust her advice and instincts and couldn't have been more pleased when she was willing to work with us. The down-in-the-trenches work is done by the Project Editor, Anne Goebel. We have enjoyed her professionalism and inputs in this process. She has been a pleasure to work with.

A special thanks to my mother, Dorothy "Bunny" Holden, who has become a great negotiator and always been a great Mom.

About the Author

Dr. Reed K. Holden is the founder and CEO of Holden Advisors (www.holdenadvisors.com), a firm that specializes in pricing and sales effectiveness. He is the co-author of the second and third editions of *The Strategy and Tactics of Pricing* and *Pricing with Confidence*, two of the leading books in the field. For the past 20 years, he has worked globally with sales and executive teams in a wide range of industries to improve their pricing performance. Contact him at Rholden@holdenadvisors.com.

Reed lives in Concord, Massachusetts, with his wife Carolyn and two golden retrievers Sam and Red.

Introduction

Selling is not as fun as it used to be. That unarguable fact takes its toll on sales professionals and the organizations they represent. If you're reading this, a good chance exists that you're a sales pro who once loved his job. How are you feeling about it today, and more importantly, have you taken a hit on your ability to deliver results? Maybe it's the way you wake up every day wondering where that great get-up-and-go feeling got up and went. Clients put you through the wringer with ever-increasing demands. They organize more and more people to participate in buying decisions. You are put through never-ending rounds of negotiation. More concessions are always demanded, and then even if you score a sale, where's the celebration?

The world is a cost-cutting one for sales professionals. Even salespeople with the *most* valuable products and services—those hand-picked by the CEO or CFO—are now negotiated with an economic buyer, better known as *procurement*.

Dealing with procurement is the new normal. To sell effectively in this economy, sales professionals must recognize that the steps of the well-crafted sales cycle have changed. The sales cycle is longer and harder to assess. Customers offer less information and demand more. Until recently, customers in a business-to-business (B2B) sale expected to negotiate and offer discounts with the reward of more volume. Salespeople developed relationships with customers over time, developed a more intimate view of their needs, could antici-pate their needs, and earned a measure of trust. In other words, you established yourself as a preferred vendor, with a badge that gave you the freedom to walk the halls of their offices. Now all bets are off.

Although your relationship buyer might still work closely with you, he usually has a new partner—procurement—that runs interference. The proposal might even still be vetted with your closest relationship contact, but that contact no longer makes the decision. Off it goes for another vetting with parties who are not invested in a partnership with you. Rather, they are motivated and compensated to cut costs and save their company as much money as possible. In this fact lies the source of many of the difficulties faced by sales professionals since the recession of 2008 changed the sales playing field.

Procurement teams have been in place and trained to drive tough negotiations for years. They prepare, and even tear apart, the financial statements of suppliers to determine what price the salesperson *should* offer, and they get it with hard-nosed negotiating tactics. Their tactical playbooks have been developed over years of practice "working over" salespeople just like you.

Salespeople who are not prepared for these professionals are often blindsided. The procurement contact might be the nicest person in the world and might even reveal the price point you need to ink the deal. She tests you to see how easily you will meet that price. Now you think you have an easy win. What you might not realize is that now that she knows how easily you dropped your price, she expects that even more discounts can be wrung out of you before she gives you the order.

Are you desperate and up against the wall because it is quarter-end? Do you need to close business whatever the price or cost to your company? Will you cave and give big price discounts? Let me ask you a few questions: Do you know how and why your price is what it is? Can you defend it? Can you demonstrate value that aligns with that price? Do you know whether the cost basis is real and competitive? If you don't know these things, you need to step back and figure them out because price negotiations are going to just get tougher. You need to understand why your prices are the levels they are and what they mean to your company's profitability. You need to know your competitors, how they perform relative to you, and what their price levels are.

Making the decision on how to price a deal is critical, and it needs to be backed up with sound reasoning. I have spent years as a pricing advisor and want to help you better manage the final frontier of good pricing—the customer negotiation. That's what this book offers.

"What separates great salespeople from good ones?" I was giving a lecture on the sales negotiation process when the student raised her hand and asked this important question. I've heard variants of this question many times. The typical phrasing is, "What separates a good salesperson from an average one?" But she asked me what distinguishes truly great salespeople from the good ones who consistently make quota and are welcome on any sales team in the world. I told her that the issue comes down to two things: knowledge and trust. The salesperson's understanding of the customer and his needs demonstrates knowledge. The experience that allows the customer to be confident that the salesperson can be relied upon to act on the customer's long-term interests instead of the salesperson's short-term ones demonstrates trust.

Prospective customers can sense immediately whether you know enough about their needs to be able to offer appropriate solutions. *Good* salespeople use their limited time with prospects to sell them on everything a product or service can do, with unsurprising hit-or-miss results. *Great* salespeople have an uncanny ability to zero in on the specific feature about which the customer cares most. How do they identify what it is? Aha!—that's what separates the great from the merely good. They use a combination of active listening and talking to people with specific knowledge of the customer.

I was speaking at a conference recently when a salesperson I've known over the years approached me. "Can I ask your advice?" he said. "I have a big sales appointment coming up." The salesperson explained that it had taken him more than a year to schedule this sales call and he didn't understand what he was getting into. I congratulated him for getting the appointment and listened as he described the situation. The prospect was a billion-dollar warehouse and storage company. I knew from my contacts in the industry that this company was most interested in increasing its return on invested capital. The salesperson was selling a software tool designed to manage warehouse and storage utilization. He wanted to emphasize the internal cost savings that his software solution could generate. I asked the salesperson two questions:

1. How much first-year savings can you realistically deliver?
2. Can your software help the company track its unused capacity?

The answer to the first question was "half a million dollars." The answer to the second was "yes."

Now, half a million dollars in cost savings is nothing to sneeze at even for a billion-dollar company. Nevertheless, I thought the cost-savings benefit was secondary to the main problem the prospect was interested in addressing. As I saw it, the company had all this underutilized storage and warehouse space sitting around. If the software could help the company increase the utilization of this non-performing space and perhaps avoid or delay building new warehouse facilities, its savings would be in the hundreds of millions of dollars. I suggested the salesperson pitch the ability of his software package to identify, track, and exploit unused capacity. The cost savings could be treated as an added bonus.

What made him a great salesperson? He really wanted to understand his customer's needs and to build trust. Asking for help was the first step. A salesperson who resists asking for help will never be great. If he had gone into the sales meeting pushing the cost savings, he would have fallen flat on his face. Worse, he would have undermined trust and sabotaged his credibility, making it more difficult for him to sell the decision makers on the features they might really care about. By seeking out someone knowledgeable about the industry, he increased his chances of making the sale. I wished him well and asked for a report on the outcome of the sales call. Although there are never guarantees in sales, he called a few weeks later to report success. He had emphasized the ability of his software to increase the warehouse company's utilization of invested capital, and the prospect had turned into a customer.

Why did I recount this story? For one simple reason—I wrote this book to help sales professionals. I want you to know that I've been where you are—I've knocked on doors and I've dialed for dollars. On the other end of the sales spectrum, I have been part of sales presentations that required months of analysis, preparation, and rehearsal. More recently, I've watched the emergence of a procurement function that has added more complexity and uncertainty to the buying center. So as you read this book, please remember that you have a guide who has worked as a sale professional and then developed an internationally recognized expertise in pricing. In 2008, I wrote *Pricing with Confidence: 10 Ways to Stop Leaving Money on the Table*.

Now with this book, I identify key insights, practices, and tools required for success in the procurement sales environment in which we operate. The following chapters offer actionable tactics and strategies to make you a more effective salesperson. That's my promise to you. Now, before I introduce the main themes of the book, allow me to tell you a bit about my sales background.

My first job after school was in sales. Like most people, my career went from job to job, but I always liked selling. There's something very satisfying about learning how to read people, ask effective questions, and close business. Looking back on my sales experience, I can now see that I was mostly wandering around in the dark. I know this because at one point in my career, I decided to be a college instructor and actually teach some of the skills that salespeople need. That decision required me to go back to school to get a doctorate degree. I focused my studies and research on buyer-seller relationships. Conducting this research was an eye-opening experience because although

I was a fairly successful salesperson, I came to understand how little I actually knew about the dynamics of selling, pricing, building trust, and the unconscious motivators of buyers and sellers. The biggest of these motivators, I learned, was trust. Without trust, leveraging the value your company creates for its customers is impossible—and a sale is nothing but a price discussion.

I'm fortunate that in my early years of selling, I had two great managers who taught me how to sell and also taught me to have enough confidence to get the job done without unnecessary discounting. The first was Fred Vorlander. He wanted me to have good technical skills and work hard to meet with customers and find opportunities, but he never put pressure on me to close business at the end of a month—it's just not the way he worked. At Exxon Information Systems, I really learned how to prospect and close a deal. I can still see my branch manager, Jack McGloin, staring me in the face saying "So what?" to push me to get my presentations crisper. He put a lot of pressure on sellers to close deals at the end of the month, but because we couldn't discount the gear, we had to learn to sell without price being an issue—even for large sales. Both jobs were great learning experiences.

It's Not Just Academic

In 1995, I decided to take a leave of absence from my teaching career to put my ideas about trust and value to work. Being in academia is nice, but I missed the rough-and-tumble of the real world. Plus, I was curious whether the material I was teaching had any relevance in sales situations where actual dollars were on the line. I saw a market opportunity in a consultancy that focused on helping companies price the products and services they introduce to the market. So there I was: an ex-professor, now a consultant. In other words, I was a salesperson once again.

I spent months beating the bushes, making cold calls, responding to requests for proposals (RFPs), and searching for clients. I had some dark moments when I regretted giving up the security of academia, but then I hit pay dirt. One of the first clients we signed was Digital Equipment Corp. (DEC, later acquired by Compaq and eventually Hewlett-Packard). DEC, based in Maynard, Massachusetts, was one of the golden stars of the burgeoning minicomputer industry. It was a heady time. DEC's products, software, and services competed furiously for customers in a rapidly changing market. The pricing issues were complex and kept me on my toes. I learned more about pricing and sales in those years than at any other point in my career. DEC seemed happy with my performance, and it seemed to me that we had a mutually respectful relationship.

After some months, however, something shifted. I slowly began to realize that DEC's procurement people were trying to take advantage of me. I had agreed to do a certain project at a negotiated price. That's how consultants operate. DEC seemed satisfied with the services my firm was providing, yet the procurement people used the contracting process to demand that we not only deliver extra services but do it for less money. The procurement manager implied that if we didn't accept DEC's new terms, the company would move its business elsewhere. I struggled with what to do because I was afraid of losing the firm's biggest client. I first got depressed and then I got angry. After all, we had a contract! I thought about calling a lawyer and fighting them in court.

I'm glad I didn't. The reason I didn't is because one day I had an epiphany—I realized it wasn't personal. Also, I understood that it takes two sides to have a conflict. What if, instead of going in and fighting, I withdrew? Would backing off work better than going in swinging? A few weeks later, I had an opportunity to test my theory.

We had agreed to start a pricing project on behalf of a new DEC product. The request for the work had come from Susan (not her real name), a senior executive with whom I had good relations. She asked us to deliver the project on a rush basis, something we were good at. That's one reason Susan reached out to us. She saw value in our ability to respond immediately. We quickly developed a budget and time frame for the work. Susan agreed with our terms, and we began the work even before we signed the agreement. That's what you're supposed to do in a trusting relationship.

About halfway into the project, I received a call from a manager in DEC's procurement department. Jerry (not his real name) trotted out a number of reasons why we had to agree to deliver the project for less money than we negotiated. I replied that we had already agreed to the terms of the engagement and we had a signed letter to that effect from Susan. Jerry chastised me for doing that. He said that I should have known that DEC's procurement policies prohibited direct negotiations with an executive and that he was going to have to renegotiate the deal.

I let a flash of anger pass over me, and then I decided to try out my new negotiating strategy of backing off. Instead of giving Jerry a piece of my mind about trust and fairness, my mind was clear. Jerry was playing a role. It was nothing personal. He was responding to certain incentives. Here's how I handled it.

I told Jerry that I was sorry we were having this conflict. I suggested that we needed to meet in person to resolve the issue, but that I couldn't make the time to do that for several weeks owing to my many commitments. This wasn't true. I really had plenty of time. We were just starting a new business and aside from the work for DEC, my biggest commitment for the next two weeks was cutting the lawn. I wanted to delay the meeting and set up Jerry to get slammed by my contact who was a senior executive. So, I further said that in the meantime, I would shut the project down (this part was true). I wasn't surprised that Jerry readily agreed with this plan. He thought I was bluffing and would quickly fold my tent. I could almost see the smile on his face.

Now, let me say a word about bluffing in negotiations. A bluff is a venture into the unknown. With a bluff, you are calculating the other side will back down or not take the challenge, but if you guess wrong, you will have to walk away. You can't back down from a bluff. If you do that, your future negotiating position is destroyed because the other party will not only conclude that you are always bluffing but that you are a coward. Strategically, bluffing is safest when you have nothing to lose, a situation that certainly didn't describe our position with DEC—but here's the thing: Although I have been known to bluff from time to time, in this particular case, I wasn't bluffing.

So I did exactly what I promised I would do. I shut down the project, which wasn't easy. It meant losing cash flow, and I hated telling my team to go home. I saw clearly what had to be done to preserve my relationship with DEC on terms we could live with. There is no better bluff than no bluff. If you take a position, you must be willing to see it through. Was I really willing to walk away from my biggest client? My team thought I was nuts because they all knew how critical the DEC project was to our young consulting firm, but I got them to all leave the office and not answer their phones. If that's a display of a little arrogance, I plead guilty.

My next call went to Susan, the VP who authorized the project. I left a message for her about what was going on and that we had reluctantly shut down the pricing project until we could get the terms sorted out. Susan must have called Jerry and read him the riot act because it wasn't ten minutes later that Jerry phoned me. Well, I made sure I was out to lunch, which in those years meant I was in the backyard of my house eating a peanut butter sandwich. Yes, I wanted to make Jerry sweat a bit. Over the next few hours, Jerry called six times. Our bookkeeper, Elaine took his increasingly desperate messages. I let him swing in the wind for a few hours, and then I called back. Jerry told me that the original terms were fine after all and requested that we get the consulting project back on track as quickly as possible.

This story offers a number of lessons. Sometimes you have to push back; but when you do, never take it personally and never blow your stack. In other words, be cool. In the musical *West Side Story*, the gang members receive a lesson in survival that applies equally well to those negotiating with powerful companies: "Go man, go/ But not like a yo-yo school boy/ Just play it cool, boy/ Real cool." If the gang members can be cool right before the rumble, so can you. Will negotiations always be a rumble? Of course not. But sometimes they are, and you've got to be ready to "Go man, go."

I can't emphasize this piece too much. Don't ever blow your stack at a procurement person or a senior executive. Above all else, keep your cool. You gain nothing by losing your temper. In many cases, procurement people actually want you to get angry and do something self-defeating. If you say anything nasty, they'll use it against you in subsequent negotiations. You will be on the defensive, agree to something you shouldn't, and end up with less power. As the saying goes, it's akin to the futility of wrestling with a pig—you both get dirty but the pig likes it. So, keep your anger in check and figure out how you can gain some level of control and maybe something that looks like retribution in the process. The best revenge is a deal on your terms.

Another lesson is that although you don't want to lose the business, you must be willing to at least act like you can put the business and the relationship on the line to get the terms you need to survive and hopefully flourish in a business. Salespeople will tell me that they can't afford to put the business on the line. That might be true, but if they act like that, procurement will see their fear and take advantage of that desperation. Instead, appear to be willing to put the business on the line—that's what I did, and it was a very effective bluff in the game.

I went on to develop and grow the consulting firm. With colleagues like Tom Nagle and Dick Harmer, I developed a proven pricing model that has been accepted by hundreds of companies around the world. Along the way, I wrote several books that included the model. These books were addressed to pricing managers and company decision-makers. This book is addressed to sales professionals and the executives who manage them.

I am proud of my first two books, but I acknowledge that neither of them address the day-to-day needs of the salespeople who feel they are out there on their own. These salespeople are in the trenches, dealing with procurement people every day of their lives. Sure, plenty of books exist about selling to companies, getting companies to be loyal, and how to better negotiate, but they all assume one thing— that one model works for all customers.

The problem is that no one-size-fits-all selling model exists. Further, procurement people often know those selling models better than salespeople, and they also know how to short-circuit attempts to develop great relationships and instead get lower and lower prices. In many high-value industries, such as professional services, medical equipment, and software, those short circuits cause companies to lose hard-earned margins and leave money on the negotiating table. That's not good business. This book shows you how to recognize and avoid getting shocked by the procurement's attempts to short-circuit relationships you have with other executives based on trust and the value your firm can provide. You've got to be ready for this and act properly so you don't undermine your relationships, value, or price.

I spent a lot of time in my academic career measuring trust in buyer-seller relationships. I conducted a lot of interviews with procurement people. The research examined trust in seven different industries offering both high- and low-tech products. I studied what analysts had to say on the importance of strategic buying and developing good relationships with suppliers. The results were not surprising: Who would argue with the proposition that definite value exists in creating and maintaining trust with strategic suppliers?

I know many procurement people who operate on this belief and work toward building good, even great, high-trust relationships with their suppliers. They are professionals who treat their suppliers with

respect. Unfortunately, given the demands of the globalized economy, these professionals are increasingly in the minority. More and
more, procurement is the place in the organization where bullies tend
to congregate. The reality today is that 80 percent of procurement
managers give the other 20 percent a bad name.

Yes, negotiations can be intense, and procurement managers can
be deceptive, but is that necessarily unethical? After all, salespeople
on the other side of the table indulge in the same gamesmanship.
So let's take a minute and talk about ethics and honesty. I recently
attended a class on advanced procurement tactics to help prepare for
this book. It was put on by a national association of procurement professionals of which I am a member. The instructor started the class
by saying that purchasing professionals should practice high ethical
behavior; there should be no substitute for truth and honesty. These
high-minded words stuck with me. The professor then moved the discussion from ethics into tactics and described a rich inventory of tricks
and swindles to use against salespeople to gain concessions. Some of
these tactics seemed deceptive to me and certainly contradicted his
earlier pronouncements about ethics and honesty. I challenged the
session leader on this inconsistency. All he could do was mumble a
weak answer.

As much as professors and instructors like to believe that procurement people should employ only practices that are ethical, in the real
world procurement is a highly Darwinian process, long in tooth and
red of claw.

Last year my consulting company was hired by a company in Australia to better understand the problems their managers were having dealing with clients that decided to run the relationship through
procurement. After a significant number of discussions with both
procurement people and people who were managing complex buyer
relationships, we developed a buyer behavior model that identified
and addressed a comprehensive matrix of selling scenarios that salespeople encounter today. Further, the model we developed not only

identifies the selling scenarios but provides specific counter-tactics appropriate to each scenario.

This powerful selling model is the main subject of this book. It is a consolidation of earlier research and numerous interviews with procurement people, salespeople, and senior executives who are dealing with what we have come to call the "procurement pricing buzz saw." It's about selling to a wide range of customers from large to small and a large number of products from commodity electronics to extremely high-value financial services, but you don't have to take my word for it. In the following pages, you will encounter a variety of examples and case histories that support both the model and the advice. Even then, you will probably want to see whether the model adds value to your particular selling challenge. I believe you will be encouraged by the power of my model to help you both meet quota *and* protect your margins.

Part I

The Great Game of Procurement

The first eight chapters of the book focus on the tricks procurement people or economic buyers use to get lower prices and how to mitigate the damage of those negotiations. This part describes the dangers of desperation pricing, applying better game tactics, and begins to introduce you to the four buying behaviors and several of the eight selling scenarios. The broad objective of the game, of course, is to avoid discounting so you can serve the customer while protecting your margins.

1

Tough Selling—The New Normal

The toughest challenge that business-to-business sales professionals and leaders face today is dealing with the margin-draining games played by the economic or procurement buyer to gain additional discounts. These traps are a part of every purchasing training manual and have been fine-tuned over the years to drain maximum discounts out of even the largest and most sophisticated suppliers.

These professionals don't use the product and apparently don't care about the supplying company, the quality or value of its products and services, or the level of trust in the company's relationship with its salespeople.

The story of the CEO of a high-quality software company seems to be the best example of dealing with this type of buyer. His sales team spent considerable time qualifying and understanding the needs of a large global technology customer and developed great relationships with the committee of customer managers who had been tasked with making the purchasing decision. The team convinced the committee that it had the best solution in terms of value and price. The team had apparently closed the deal.

Suddenly a manager from purchasing showed up and asked the CEO, "Do you know what the stomp is? It's when the big customer stomps the vendor." He sent a clear signal that the deal wasn't concluded until a cascading series of discounts and concessions were extracted from the company. And that's how the deal went down. The discounts were given, concessions were made, and finally the deal was done. The sad part is that it didn't have to happen like that.

This story is being repeated in too many situations throughout the global business community. There was a time when this type of procurement behavior was relegated to commoditized manufacturing businesses such as automobile sales, but it has now spread to the sales of high-value medical devices and professional services. This is the decade of the rise of purchasing, or the economic buyer. These buyers are taking control and driving prices down using every tactic in their well-developed playbook until they are successful in meeting their cost cutting goals and earning a place at the executive table. This state of affairs is the "new normal."

Because of this pricing pressure, high-quality, high-value large companies aren't covering their cost of capital. Profits are draining from once-profitable businesses and companies are going out of business because they don't know how to deal with the "purchasing pricing buzz saw."

One tactic to combat the preceding is to invest in training salespeople to understand customer value and develop better relationships with their customers. Over the past decade companies have been spending more and more dollars on training salespeople. Some estimates point to yearly training budgets of $1,000–$1,200 per salesperson. With an estimate of 15 million salespeople in the U.S. alone, that's a lot of training dollars. This segment of training is also one of the fastest-growing service segments, with an estimated growth of 10 percent in 2011 alone. However, the cost of the training is small compared to the wasted time and unnecessary discounting that occurs because the training doesn't prepare salespeople for effectively dealing with the pricing games that purchasing people play today.

All these efforts around understanding value and developing relationships are wasted on the hard-hearted economic buyers and the games they play to get lower prices. That economic buyer is usually a purchasing professional, but she might also be a department manager or even a senior executive who is being coached by a purchasing professional on how to get high value for low prices. The list of tactics to bluff and win against the hapless salesperson is long and well known. The problem is that nothing in the relationship or value-oriented sales training programs can help salespeople deal with the economic buyer and the games they play.

In fact, many of the training programs teach tactics that fall right into the traps that purchasing professionals use to get high-value products and services for low prices. Just the simple *threat* of putting the business out to bid is often enough to drain dramatic price discounts from a salesperson who is just trying to satisfy the customer. Why? Because salespeople have been trained that customer satisfaction is very important.

If the threat is not enough, another common tactic is to *actually* put the purchase out to bid, qualifying several vendors that are in truth, unacceptable to the customer. They are Rabbits—there simply to drive the price of the preferred vendor or the Advantaged Player down as low as possible. This practice has always been true of commoditized products and industries, but it is now occurring in highly differentiated areas such as software, professional services, and medical equipment.

There was a time when only the big guys, the marquee-named companies, seemed to have all the advantages. They used their scale and brand to squeeze the little guy. Now even medium and small buyers have learned the tactics of the mighty and squeeze their suppliers. Even large, world-class suppliers in high-value industries services are seeing their margins shrink due to run-ins with procurement. This situation is not going to go away when the recession ends. Buyers have learned to get lower prices and will continue to use that power until vendors figure out a way to blunt those efforts with better tactics of their own.

Company-Supported Sales Traps to Avoid

Many tactics can cause salespeople to drop price. Salespeople can learn about those tactics, but before they can successfully play the game needed to ensure increased revenue and profits, they must understand some things that their own companies do that undermine a salesperson's ability to successfully negotiate with a customer. The following sections describe them.

Encouraging Desperation Pricing

In the 1987 film *Broadcast News*, there's a line I like. The failed anchorman played by Albert Brooks says, "Wouldn't this be a great world if insecurity and desperation were attractive qualities?" The reality is that procurement managers are drawn to insecurity and desperation like blood draws sharks. So the first thing salespeople and executives must be able to do is manage their desperation. Having so much faith in the value of your products or services that desperation doesn't even come into play is a better tactic. If you must be desperate, though, for Pete's sake don't show it.

Not showing desperation isn't easy. Desperation comes from something even more scary—measurement. Salespeople have objectives. Executives have Wall Street. Objectives are the ante to get into the game of winning business. They are not just objectives, but hard-to-obtain objectives called sales quotas. Furthermore, the sales quotas are easily measurable. All business people know that they have to hit their numbers. When was the last time you heard of a human resources manager being fired for not making his or her numbers? Salespeople are a special category; they live and die by their numbers—weekly, monthly, quarterly, and yearly. Their compensation is directly related to the last set of numbers. If they slip one month, salespeople know they might have a month or so to make up the difference. If they let it slip much more than that, they know that they are history. Among sales professionals, this reality breeds a certain kind of desperation. When procurement people sense desperation, watch out. All bets are off.

Even if desperation is not there, many procurement people have figured out how to create it. The easiest trick a buyer has is to delay a purchase. The longer they can wait, the more desperate salespeople and their managers become. Because procurement managers know that most salespeople are on monthly quotas, they have learned to wait until the end of the month in the hope that the salesperson will accept virtually any price just so he doesn't miss his quota. This trick is well known to consumers. Heck, even my 89-year-old mother used that trick a few years ago by visiting a car dealership toward the end of the month when salespeople are increasingly desperate to meet their quotas. There was no selling, no thought of value regarding convenience and service. She got a great deal, and it was the first car she had ever purchased!

I wish that this desperation game were simply a tactic created by procurement people, imposed on sales professionals from one end of the negotiating table. However, the sad reality is that desperation often has its origins from the same side of the table that the salesperson occupies. How many times have you been pressured to hit your numbers at the end of the month and quarter? How many times have you seen a manager or senior executive travelling through your territory trying to close business to make the end-of-period numbers? It happens every day. The point is that this type of desperation makes salespeople lousy negotiators because they are too desperate to close a deal and are willing to suffer procurement tactics to get the order.

Succumbing to the "White Horse Syndrome"

I have a name for what happens when sales managers come into the field to "help" the sales reps. I call it the "White Horse Syndrome" to honor the well-intended objectives of the executives. They actually believe their actions are akin to the hero who jumps on a white steed, rides out into the untamed territory, and single-handedly saves the town from the bad guys. The reality is not only do they undermine the sales rep calling on the procurement manager, but they also telegraph even more desperation on the part of the company. Their big weapon? Just a bigger discount.

I learned this lesson some years ago when I was the new marketing manager of a medium-sized technology company. We weren't hitting our numbers. A few days before the end of my third month, the division president (let's call him Bill), paid me a visit in my office. He suggested that I offer a 10 percent discount for large-volume orders as an incentive for us to meet end-of-period numbers. I quickly agreed. After all, he was the boss and I was new—I just didn't know any better. We offered the discount and—guess what?—we hit our numbers that month.

The entire marketing team went out to celebrate, and I was feeling good, but then I closely monitored sales activity for the following weeks. Sales were plummeting. They didn't just get soft, they evaporated. They were as low as Gandhi's cholesterol. So I made some inquiries and quickly figured out what was happening. The 10 percent discount we offered went to our distributors. Now, distributors don't actually consume products. They simply store them and distribute the products to customers who use them in the production of products and then sell those products to the people or companies who finally use them. It's that last activity—coming back for more—that most marketing efforts should focus on.

All our end-of-month discount did was to encourage the distributors to load up the channel. The discount did nothing to encourage sales by the only constituency that matters—the end customers. With the distribution channel loaded, the distributors just sat back until their inventory needed replenishing—something that the low demand for our product predicted would be some months in the future.

You can guess what happened next. At the end of the month, Bill paid me another visit and suggested we extend and increase the discount. But by now I had learned my lesson and I trotted out all the arguments for why this strategy was unsustainable and would do nothing but erode margins. Bill listened carefully, nodding his head as if he understood, and then ordered me to again offer the month-end discount.

This time, even with the discount, we failed to meet our sales goals. The channel—apparently still stuffed from the previous month—couldn't handle any more, nor would it open up until we figured out how to increase real sales to actual customers who would consume the product. Actually, the truth was worse than that, but it would take another month to figure it out.

A month after that, Bill again dropped by, suggesting I approve another discount. This time I held my ground, and we had a spirited conversation about the matter. The upshot is that I won the argument. We put our marketing efforts into demonstrating our value to the customers to stimulate orders and empty the distribution channel. We did that pretty well because something else happened. I started getting calls from our distributors asking when we were going to announce the discounts they had come to expect. This time, we didn't grant the discounts, and the business revenues returned to a reasonable and much more profitable level. The distributors had been delaying their orders in anticipation of yet another panic discount. This time, we held our ground. It had only taken us two months to train our dealers to wait until the end of the month. But I'm happy to report that it took only two months to retrain our customers to change their ordering behavior. Both our revenues and margins increased.

I won the battle but lost the war. Bill fired me a few months later because he got tired of arguing with me. Some managers just don't like being upstaged by their subordinates. Losing a job is no fun, but I learned a lot from that experience and was glad I had the confidence to do what I knew was right in serving the company and supporting my sales team. I got a better job, and Bill lost his job six months later.

There Is Hope if You Play the Game Right

Yes, salespeople and their leaders have responded by mindless discounting, hoping to make up any losses through higher volume. Unfortunately, discounting is a fool's response. Those who live and die by discounting don't live very long.

Sales professionals labor under the assumption that all the power is on the customer's side. That's because the inevitable response is price discounting. Discounting becomes an addiction that actually undermines the long-term health of the business. It decreases profits and erodes the quality of customer relationships. The sad fact is that panic discounting happens even in organizations that provide significant value to their customers. This value is overlooked, underestimated, or flat out ignored when, in fact, it is the key to breaking free of the conventional wisdom of folding your cards and just discounting.

To the extent sales professionals believe they must trade margins for revenues, they undermine the success of their business, which needs profits more than revenue to survive. To make matters worse, they train their customers to expect a price concession each and every negotiation. They validate the tactics that customers use, and they fall into the procurement pricing trap each and every time.

Vendors have a number of tricks and tactics available to fight back, protect their margins, and keep the business. Negotiating in these customer situations is not supposed to be surrender. Remember, the bigger they are, the bigger their appetite. This is true for both suppliers *and* customers. The big secret is that procurement is sweating the deal just as much as you are, but they just learned not to show it. They have learned how to bluff in the big poker game of purchasing, and they know that their bluff will work each and every time.

The name of the game today is maintaining margins. To do that, you must outplay the games of procurement. A way exists for salespeople to blunt the price focus of procurement professionals and not fall prey to their tactics. A way exists for them to assess the "game" the customer is playing and adopt tactics that preserve precious profits from mindless discounting. A way exists for business executives to provide the direction and support that allows salespeople to be effective players in the great game of procurement.

The way is to consider the negotiation with the economic buyer as a game of poker. The game has positions that the seller will fulfill. Based on that position, specific tactics exist that can preserve profits and resources. Those tactics redefine the game so that value can be leveraged, discounts can be minimized, and orders can be closed at price levels that are fair to both parties.

Consider the game of the Advantaged Player—that salesperson is at the negotiating table with a customer. Other players (competitors) are probably also at the table, and the buyer spends a lot of time talking about how the other competitors' prices are much lower than the Advantaged Player's. In fact, some yelling might be going on about how the Advantaged Player has to lower prices to close the deal. Does he have to? Nope—it's all a poker game. In fact, the more yelling that occurs, the worse the hand—for the customer. The Advantaged Player has the winning hand. He doesn't have to discount; he just has to play the game and close the deal.

Fred was a junior partner in a professional services firm negotiating with the CEO of one of his clients to do $300,000 worth of consulting work. The company was a long-term client, and Fred had a good relationship with the CEO. The CEO said that he would agree to let Fred do the work if he dropped the price to $200,000. Fred knew that the company needed to get the work done and that his firm was the best one to do it. He knew that he was an Advantaged Player and held to his price. The CEO, who was just trying to test Fred, placed the order for the work two weeks later—at the full price.

Compare Fred's position to the position of the Rabbit—that is, the salesperson who is added to the bid list to drive down the price of the Advantaged Player. The Rabbit has no chance of winning the business. He has no contacts with the real decision maker and no chance to sell value. The Rabbit has the losing hand and is better off just not playing the game, especially if the time needed to prepare a bid is more than two minutes. It's just a flat waste of his time.

Consider Sally, who was a business development person with a global general contracting firm that specialized in design build for chemical plants. She had been trying to do work with a global pharmaceutical firm and was frustrated that she could never get beyond the purchasing department. One day, her contact asked whether she was interested in bidding on a new plant being built in India. Of course, she was interested. She assembled a team that worked for two months putting together a proposal to do the work. It was gorgeous and provided everything the customer asked for. She even had the lowest price. But that only lasted until the potential client convinced its preferred supplier to match the price. Sally lost the order and wasted hundreds of thousands of dollars' worth of time and effort pursuing a piece of business she had no chance of winning. That's the game of the Rabbit.

The preceding examples describe two of the games salespeople and executives play in the great game of procurement. There are eight easy-to-identify games and tactics associated with each one. If you understand your position in the game, you can play the game better—walking away from the table if you have a losing hand but outbluffing the customer if you have the winning hand. Playing the game properly is not that hard, and it's a heck of a lot more fun. It does require a concerted effort of both salespeople and executives who are committed to understanding the game and using the right tactics to make sure they protect profits and revenue along the way.

2

The Tells of the Game

Bluffing is a key element of any game of chance with multiple players involved. The same is true in the great game of procurement. A *tell* is a little sign that another player might give that indicates the nature of his bluff. Salespeople need to recognize a tell for what it is—part of a bluff. It shouldn't be taken at face value; instead, it should be interpreted by the salesperson as part of the bluff. The procurement professional's job is to get the best deal from vendors. To accomplish this, many have adopted well-honed tricks of the trade to ensure they do that. It's not a profession for the fastidious or the faint-hearted. Salespeople must know how to recognize and defend themselves against all the tactics and tricks used by procurement professionals. Some of these include

- Representations that all bids will be considered when the successful vendor has already been decided

- Indiscriminate throwing of terms into a contract to see which ones will stick

- Representing that an agreement is concluded only to reopen negotiations in an effort to extract even better terms

- Changing the terms and deadlines of a negotiation to unbalance the other side

- "My way or the highway" statements that let sellers know they don't care which company wins the business

- Blatant dishonesty or bullying to get terms, discounts, and concessions
- Abuse of their suppliers' time and trust

This book can help readers recognize procurement's traps and minimize their exposure to unscrupulous procurement managers. Good selling companies will continue to invest in innovation, supply chain improvement, and account relationships at their own risk, but those that are smart will do it selectively, based on the way they are treated and when and how they can see a good return in terms of sales and profits for their efforts. They also must remember that they are not powerless. In 2008, when Chrysler started breaking contracts with its suppliers, the suppliers stopped shipping and shut Chrysler down within weeks. Suppliers actually exist who have recognized that a) they don't want to get pushed around as much as they do by customers and b) they have considerably more power than they thought. Until salespeople take their place as equals at the bargaining table, they will continue to be victims of procurement's agenda of abuse.

Before a negotiation, your job is to understand your value and power in the process. During the negotiation, you need to recognize the tricks and tactics that procurement and customer senior executives play to get you to drop price. This book shows you not only how to identify the tactics, but also how to plan and respond appropriately. Value is the true look at how you are different than competitors. If you don't know your value, and more importantly your difference relative to a competitor, or have little confidence in that value during negotiations, why should your negotiating partner in procurement? In many cases, their game is more of a test of your confidence in your price and your value. It's a test of your backbone!

Recognizing "Tells"

Rather than just reacting to what you see and hear during a negotiation, first analyze all of it from the standpoint of being in a game. If they say your product or service is a commodity, recognize it's part of a game. If they say that five competitors are bidding, even if it is the case, recognize that all of those suppliers are not equal. When a user or budget sponsor has agreed to terms that are acceptable to you and then procurement gets involved to unravel the agreement, recognize that it's all part of a game. Remember that as the supplier, you are there to get fair terms for your company.

To begin to recognize the game procurement people play, salespeople need to recognize the "tells" of the game. In poker a *tell* is a consistent quirk or body language—maybe an extra eye blink or sigh—that gives away that the person has a good hand or is in a strong position to bluff. Tells are the indicators that an economic buyer or procurement person is suddenly playing a game to get lower prices. In recognizing these tells, a salesperson can properly assess the selling situation or game and employ the right tactics. This is not intended to be a complete list—the best list of procurement tells come from Larry Steinmetz's book *How to Sell at Margins Higher Than Your Competitors*. The following list describes some of the tells salespeople should be wary of.

- **The Value Trap:** Has a procurement manager ever beguiled you with a statement that he or she wants the conversation to be about value? Did you smile and get excited that you might actually get a chance to leverage the value of your product or service? How did it work out? Yes, it ended up focusing on price, didn't it? The value trap is used to disarm suppliers. Despite representations about value, the agenda of procurement all along is to extract price discounts. Every time the supplier attempts to bring the discussion to the value of products and services, the procurement person changes the subject to bring the conversation to the one place he always wants it: price. The important thing to remember in this tell is that the procurement statement is responding to certain incentives that have nothing to do with the value of your product or service. They just think about value differently than you do. For some procurement people the word *value* is synonymous with price. Procurement people think about value in terms of price and subsequent cost reductions. When they are at the table with a supplier, their focus on value is high value at very low prices—and they get that by focusing on the low price. This trick is designed to get you to react in a way that is good for them and bad for you.

- **Good Cop, Bad Cop:** The good cop, bad cop tactic is one that any viewer of the TV series *Law and Order* will recognize. Two cops are in collusion to extract a confession from a suspect. The good cop comes in, seemingly reasonable and caring. The good cop offers a soda or cigarette and gently suggests the suspect would be well advised to deal with him before the bad cop comes in. Then the bad cop comes in. The bad cop is surly, mean, and unhelpful. So it is in some procurement negotiations. Your initial counterpart will be reasonable, cooperative, and pleasant. He will have good things to say about your products and customer support. His goal is for you to lower your guard. Eventually, someone identified as senior in authority to the first guy then walks in. This is the bad cop, and you can expect him to be surly, mean-spirited, critical, and generally threatening. He will ask for concessions. If you're ready for the good cop, bad cop routine, you won't be at a disadvantage. You find out more about how to respond to this in greater detail in Chapter 10, "Beware the Signs of a Losing Game," but simply put, call out the tactic. Smile and let them know that you understand their game.

- **The White Board:** A common procurement prop during a negotiation is a big white board with conspicuously legible contents. As the representative from the supplier walks in, he or she will be surprised to see the white board listed with multiple competitors and the evaluation of those competitors on different features. Inevitably, the supplier currently in the room will be number three on the list. Certainly the supplier will never occupy the number-one position. Watch out! The white board is a prop that the hosts want the supplier's rep to notice. Sometimes the hosts will act all flustered that the contents of the white board were exposed and quickly turn it to the wall. All this is more theater. Sometimes it's a quote in the form of a letter from a competitor strategically placed on a procurement person's desk. Whatever the form, the white board is nothing more than a distraction designed to shake up the supplier prior to negotiations. So when you enter the negotiation room and see the white board trick, just ignore it. Nothing of significance is on the board for you to glean. The scene is all designed to distract you from the real point: If you're at the table, they think you offer value, and you are the preferred vendor.

Evaluating Procurement's Position

Suppose a customer is getting ready to place an order and suddenly procurement gets involved. That is not necessarily the time for sales to panic and assume that they're going to have to lower the price. The main question for sales to answer is, "Is this a logistical development in which procurement is involved merely to process the paperwork, or is it getting involved to put the vendor through the discounting wringer?" Three variations exist that predict outcome and give sales professionals a sense of the role that procurement will play:

- **Rubber Stamp:** Procurement is just going to confirm what someone else has already agreed to and issue a purchase order in confirmation. This outcome is common in sales of high-risk process systems when you are dealing with a senior operational manager and for professional services when you are dealing with a senior executive, especially the CEO. Procurement does what most senior executives want—if they say to issue the purchase order (PO), then procurement will issue the PO with no hesitation.

- **Terms and Conditions:** With this next level, procurement is working on contract terms. Although this outcome isn't likely to turn into a pricing discussion, sellers need to be careful that unfavorable terms don't slip into the contract. Many procurement professionals have learned that if they throw a number of terms into the contract at this point, some terms will be challenged, and others will find their way into the final language. They might include 50 terms they don't care about with the hope that the two or three terms they consider important slip through. The risk here for sales is that they become so excited about closing an order that they allow those terms to slip through, to the seller's regret some months or years down the line. The trick in dealing with this type of procurement is for sales to have the appropriate people review and fine-tune the contract. At this point, the vendor should remember that it has a fair amount of leverage. After all, the buyer has decided that it's in their best interest to do business with the vendor. This situation gives the preferred vendor considerable power to push back or to refuse some of the terms. Often, the terms represent a test; the procurement people or legal department want to see what they can get away with.

- **Absolute Control:** When procurement takes absolute control of a purchase, then the sales professionals know they are playing poker. Chapter 8, "Negotiating with Poker Players," addresses the specific techniques to address this situation. For now, let me emphasize that the most important thing is to keep one's cool and resist the urge to take it personally. In *Getting Past No: Negotiating in Difficult Situations*, William Ury suggests that the salespeople "go to the balcony" when the gamesmanship goes into overdrive. By this, Ury means take a self-imposed timeout and cool off when the procurement people suddenly start making demands. I concur. The tactics in this phase of the sales process are designed to rattle the salespeople. So I suggest that when procurement takes absolute control of the process, that is the time for sales professionals to take absolute control of their emotions. Discipline is required from everyone on the sales side. I know this lesson from first-hand experience.

Getting a sense of procurement's level of control helps you to craft a sales approach that on the surface accommodates procurement's needs but also can set you up to regain control of the process. I had one situation with a client with whom I had gone through a long process of qualification and approval. A procurement person suddenly inserted herself into the process and started negotiating to drive down the price. I recount the details of this story in Chapter 4, "Getting the Tactics Right the First Time," but for now, let me just say that when the deal was finally inked, no procurement person was in the picture. My point is that just because procurement people get involved and adopt a high level of control over the process doesn't mean that they necessarily stay involved. If you follow the rules in Chapter 4 and play the game well, no reason exists for procurement to have the same level of control at the end of the negotiation as it attempts to have at the beginning.

Dealing with Procurement Styles

The issue of procurement style is another determinant of the game being played and the optimum selling strategy. Think of procurement styles as falling into three basic categories: collegial, professional, and kamikaze.

- **Collegial:** Procurement people who are friendly and open can indicate one of several possibilities. The most likely possibility is that the vendor will enjoy a collegial and mutually rewarding relationship with the customer. Even so, some salespeople fall into a trap. Lulled into a false sense of complacency, the salespeople might not be aware when the customer is planning to run a "good cop, bad cop" swindle. Taking the relationship at face value is usually a good idea—that is, until some of the tells begin to crop up, which indicate that the games have begun.

- **Professional:** Professional procurement people are great to deal with. They have no hidden agenda. They tell their vendors what they need to know in order to serve the customer. Yes, professional procurement people tend to be quite controlling, but that doesn't mean they will be a problem—they are often just trying to do their job in the imperfect world of business. If procurement is indifferent to whether a vendor bids or not, it means that the customer has sufficient vendors.

- **Kamikaze:** Kamikaze refers to the yelling and screaming, the threats, and the manipulation that procurement people sometimes resort to. These guys are definitely into rattling the salespeople sitting across the table. Their goal is to get the salespeople off-center, so they shift the focus from margins (which is the only place it should rightly be) and get so flummoxed they end up doing something silly. At this point, salespeople should remember the admonition, "Go to the balcony." Consider the story of a procurement manager—I'll call Jim. He went kamikaze on a sales team that had the audacity (in Jim's view) to charge 13 percent more for a semiconductor than the closest competitor. I was consulting for the sales team, so I had intimate knowledge of the negotiations. The sales team had done its homework and knew its product offered unique value both in the feature set it offered as well as the service component attached to it. Jim's position was that the product was a commodity and there was no legitimate reason to charge a premium. The sales team stuck to its position and was willing to walk away from the deal. The result? Jim caved and closed the deal at the premium level. The sales team succeeded because it realized two things. First, it understood it was playing a game. Second, it understood their company was Jim's preferred vendor. Having that knowledge meant that Jim's kamikaze attempts were launched in vain. The team didn't panic and closed a very large and profitable deal.

Recognize that procurement style and position are not always connected. We've seen some procurement people take absolute control yet have a very collegial, friendly style. We've also seen kamikaze behavior on the simple rubber stamping of order terms. The point is that these are both indicators of the kind of game you're playing and point to the tactics you should be using to gain some level of control over the process.

3

Stacking the Deck in Your Favor

Negotiation between salespeople and procurement is similar to gambling in many ways. Success in both customer negotiations and gambling requires good information, steely nerves, patience, and most of all, the ability to stay cool. When negotiators get emotional, they lose. Much of the gamesmanship by procurement is intended to get sellers to lose their cool. In both contexts, the negotiator who is more in control of his or her emotions wins.

Have you ever been in a casino? It offers many games and many tables. Veteran gamblers know the odds of winning at each table and choose based on their own appetite for risk and reward. Although there are many variables, one constant is ever present. Wagering, like a customer negotiation, is a zero-sum game. That is, every dime that ends up in one pocket is taken out of another. Both customer negotiations and gambling involve bluffing and an imperfect understanding of the opponent's motivations and what cards he's holding. Both disciplines require the confidence to know when, as the Kenny Rogers' song goes, "to hold 'em, when to fold 'em, when to walk away, and know when to run."

You need to think about preparing for the negotiating game at four levels: the individual salesperson, his managers, the internal company systems and metrics of his company, and finally the customer. To be a good negotiator, the individual salesperson must have the confidence and skills to play the game well, which takes training and experience. Heck, I've been selling for many years, and I still am learning. The salesperson's managers and the manager's manager along with the right systems need to support good negotiating. In recent years, I've seen a lot of systems and managers who undermine a salesperson's ability to negotiate well. Chapter 1, "Tough Selling—The New Normal," covers some of the "systems" problems. When we look at those four levels, things can get quite convoluted and complex. For the sake of simplicity, I'd like to start with a few pieces of advice so that when you, as a salesperson, get to the game table, you've got a better shot at winning.

This chapter provides a few pieces of advice so that salespeople can be better negotiators in this great game of procurement. So, let's dig in and see how negotiation games play out and what we as salespeople do right and do wrong.

The first thing to remember when sitting down to negotiate with a customer is that the customer dictates the game to be played. The customer, after all, has the money. The golden rule prevails. (He who has the gold makes the rules.) Customers define who they deal with, how they deal with the partners they choose, and the terms of the negotiation. The customer specifies the process of the interaction and who they let the seller deal with. Most of all, the customer selects the winner. The seller defines the game of play. Your job is to figure out that game and play it in a way that gives you the greatest likelihood of winning. I define winning as either eventually getting the business at a profitable level for your company or having the confidence to walk away from the table when the odds dramatically favor another player.

Just because the buyer determines the game doesn't mean you don't have any power. In some cases, you have considerably more power than you realize. Most games that procurement plays are designed to get salespeople to think they have less power than they do. They want salespeople to fall prey to their multiple bluffs and feel that they have to keep adding price discounts to the pot in order to keep playing.

So, get ready to prepare for your game of negotiation. Properly assessing your customer's agenda and your position so that you can employ the right tactics takes experience, insight, and work. Under-stand that when procurement is involved, preparing responses to their game tactics is important. It's perhaps even more important than the work you put into scoping the deal and building a persuasive proposal showing your value. To play properly, view it all as a game of poker. It's all about moving the odds at the table to your favor. After you do, you'll enjoy the game and get much better results in terms of revenue and lots of profit for your firm. Before we get to more specific tactics, you should know a few basic ground rules that make for better nego-tiations, as discussed next.

Understanding Your Customer's Game

Before sitting down at the negotiating table, you must deter-mine what game the customer is planning to play. That is, what is his agenda when dealing with salespeople and vendors in general? What is his agenda in the present negotiation? Watch carefully because the game dictates the rules of play. The game also dictates your position in that play. You can't put together a sales strategy—let alone justify putting the effort into actually playing the game, developing exten-sive proposals, or going through negotiations—until you have a good understanding of what the customer really wants out of the game.

I am continually amazed at how much time, effort, and money a company will put into assembling a fancy proposal without know-ing the answers to some basic questions about the customer's buying agenda. It's like going up to a slot machine that has just given a big payout knowing that for all the dollars you put in, you're not going to get anything back. Conversely, if you understand the game rules, it's like playing a slot that is hot for a big payout—profitable business for your firm. The essence of strategy is the efficient allocation of scarce resources—in your case, that is time and the involvement of others in your company. If you are going to spend time and resources on a sales cycle, then understanding the likelihood of payback to the company, which requires getting answers to a few qualifying questions, is important. Sure, for true commodity products where a proposal is a simple quotation, responding to every request for proposal (RFP) and seeing what happens might be reasonable. In this situation the customer agenda is often simple—get the lowest price. Even if the agenda is more complex, if responding is easy, then go for it. But, if it takes any effort more than a simple email response, you're better off stepping back and understanding the game before you ante up.

More than just qualifying the relationship opportunity, this qualification process is designed to assess your opportunity to win with this particular customer with this particular business opportunity. By asking a series of questions (some of which you might be uncomfortable with at first), you can figure out the nature of the game you are in, whether or not you should play it, and, if you do, how to best play the hand you are given. These questions help qualify the role and agenda of procurement as well as the competitive landscape. Here are few to consider:

- What is the process for evaluating vendors and proposals?
- What are the names and positions of everyone in the process?
- Who is the ultimate decision maker?
- How many bidders are being considered, and which companies are invited?

I'll list even more specific questions to ask when we talk about qualifying and choosing your game tactics in Chapter 4, "Getting the Tactics Right the First Time," but these are good simple starting questions that help you begin to understand and test the customer's agenda. If you don't know the answer to one or all of these questions, pack up your bags and look for another opportunity because you will be the sucker at this game. Yes, it takes backbone to ask these questions, but that is part of being a professional: asking the right questions at the right time to make sure your tactics are appropriate for the game.

Qualifying can test your confidence. It is part of determining the game you are in. Not being able to get or not knowing the information are generally bad signs, especially if you work for a firm where the strategy is to provide value and good relationships. Chances are that this is a game you can't win or you need to play it in a special way so that you get better results. Even with the information you collect, you still have more work to do. This preparation work for procurement negotiations is so critical that salespeople need to recognize it as a change or an added step in their sales process. If you use a formal selling program, this would be an added module or step in the process.

Finding Your Hidden Power

Here is one of the big secrets of procurement professionals. If a supplier is actually at the negotiating table, two things are true:

- The supplier is perceived to have value.
- The supplier is almost certainly the preferred supplier.

Even if multiple vendors are selected, the preferred vendor is usually the first one at the negotiating table. This insight is a "secret" insofar as big companies do their best to disguise its reality. It's not in the interests of procurement people for suppliers to recognize their own significance. In fact, the more *insignificant* a supplier perceives itself to be, the better it is for the buyer's company. The central goal of the procurement process is to keep suppliers sufficiently unbalanced so suppliers fail to recognize the real power that they can bring to bear on the negotiations. Procurement professionals apply a multitude of tricks and swindles to keep suppliers on the defensive. You need to understand your power in order to know when and how to react to those tricks; see Chapter 4 for more on that topic. The important point is that if you are at the table, you have power. If customers are talking to you, you have power. The knowledge of that power gives you the confidence you need to understand and react properly to their tricks.

Limiting Exposure of Senior Executives

Procurement people know that maneuvering the senior executives of their vendors to the negotiating table is to procurement's advantage. Salespeople need to resist doing that. Letting senior executives from the supplier get involved in negotiations over terms can be a mistake. Those negotiations should be left to the professionals, usually mid-level managers. When senior executives get involved, it should be to solidify existing relationships and position value—not price. If those executives are properly trained on the tactics of good negotiation and have the required confidence, they should at times lead the charge. If this isn't the case, they often do more damage than good. Procurement professionals know and want to take advantage of that.

A few years ago, we worked with a financial services sales team preparing for a renegotiation with a large global bank to determine the terms going forward of a long-standing partnership. This bank had just hired a senior team of procurement experts who were conducting discount-oriented negotiations with all of their long-term partner suppliers.

During the planning sessions for negotiations, the senior leadership for the supplier was both involved and willing to learn how to better manage the process. However, their initial tendency was to jump right in and start negotiating. I suggested that doing so would play right into the hands of the bank's procurement people. So the selling firm assigned only mid-level client-services people to attend the preparatory meetings that would expose the bank's terms and offers. I stressed that these initial meetings would be about discovery and that no decisions should be made. If senior executives were present, they might be tempted to actually decide something. Any such decisions would almost certainly be disadvantageous to the seller because the decisions would be by definition, unplanned. Unplanned decisions and those made "in the moment" are often those you regret the most later. This is where most of the mistakes are made—rushing to make unplanned decisions. Procurement people hope for that.

The bank's procurement people then requested a meeting with the selling company's President. Again, they were hoping for an unplanned decision. At my recommendation, the executive agreed to the meeting on the condition that it would be a meeting with non-procurement senior executives and the agenda would be about improving the strategic relationship between the firms. The President would simply refuse to engage in price negotiations.

The bank agreed to a meeting on the President's terms. We anticipated that the meeting would actually be a ploy and the executive would be ambushed by the bank's procurement agenda, so we did some role-playing to prepare the President for such a maneuver. Sure enough, when the meeting got started, all the non-procurement executives that were promised didn't show up, and only the procurement manager was present to lamely announce that the other attendees were unavoidably "unavailable." Having anticipated this eventuality, without drama or argument, the President simply got up and left the bank. A few weeks later, the bank and the supplier inked a new contract based on terms negotiated by the sales professionals on both sides. The selling team was able to hold its price.

So if your executives are good at understanding and arguing about value and solidifying relationships then fine, let them work with you on customers, but if they keep wanting to discount to close deals, try to get them to stay home.

Firing the Customer

It takes confident leadership for the supplier to fire the customer, but sometimes, regrettably, that is the seller's best move. It will be painful, but it's less painful than the alternatives. The story of Incredible Foods, a dessert delivery service in Gibsonia, Pennsylvania, (a suburb of Pittsburgh) is instructive. Some years ago, Incredible Foods got lucky and landed a huge customer—Starbucks—and became Starbucks' preferred vendor for crumb cake. In fact, crumb cake was the only product that Starbucks purchased. However, given the volumes of crumb cake that Starbucks ordered, the coffee giant became its biggest customer, eventually representing 48 percent of Incredible Foods' revenues. Letting one customer get so dominant is never healthy for a supplier. It inevitably leads the customer to take advantage of and actually try to dominate the vendor, which is what Starbucks did. Over the years, the big procurement guns at Starbucks negotiated the contract price points so low that Incredible Food's margins became as flaky and delicate as the crumb cake itself. Incredible Foods CEO Jim Christy had succeeded in increasing revenues by reaching a bigger market, but he discovered that more revenue doesn't necessarily translate into profit.

The problem was that Starbucks had extracted price concessions so extravagant that Incredible Foods couldn't service the account at a profit. Starbucks had been opening ten stores a year in each of its regions. Incredible Foods dedicated five trucks and drivers to the account, plus two employees who did nothing but write reports for Starbucks. The cost of fuel, insurance, and employee benefits made the whole partnership unsustainable for Incredible Foods. So Christy made the decision to cut its relationship with Starbucks. He shrank the staff by 5 percent, eliminated a sales office, sold some of the trucks, and focused the firm's marketing efforts on more local customers who negotiated deals with a handshake and generally didn't have layers of procurement people and accountants getting in the way. Christy's strategy paid off. By firing its biggest customer, Incredible Foods went from a profit of zero to 11 percent of sales in one year.

Great leadership is a key element to winning the procurement game. Firing any customer takes courage. Firing your biggest account takes extraordinary courage and leadership. If you are losing money, though, it is clearly the best thing to do. In years past, many companies took unprofitable deals or unprofitable accounts (often the marquee names) because they were confident that other, more profitable deals would make up for any initial loss. They knew they were losing money on each deal but thought they could make it up in volume.

Even in the best of economic times, this strategy is perilous. Today, with so much downward pressure on prices across the board, this strategy has even less to recommend it. Poor negotiators fall prey to the pricing buzz saw of procurement: The continual downward pressure on prices to the point where the customer is no longer profitable. It is the leadership around value and eliminating unprofitable customers that gives salespeople the courage they need to be better negotiators. That courage comes from the examples of the senior executives who don't panic, who understand their value, and who don't fall prey to the time pressures of monthly goals and the games that procurement plays. Those leaders need to be willing to stand up for their prices and walk away from customers that aren't good for the company. More often than you would expect, the customer will fold his game and come back with better terms.

Sometimes the willingness to fire a customer is enough to keep the business on terms that actually work for the supplier. I'm not saying you should actually fire the customer. I am saying that you should be willing to stick to your guns and expect that you will be treated openly and honestly. When the tricks begin, the willingness to fire the customer means that you are willing to get up and walk away from the game to make a point about how you want to be treated. You must also be willing to play games as well to blunt the effort of the economic buyer. This willingness is another benefit of bold leadership. The following simple story describes such an outcome.

Bob, a senior executive at a global telecommunications company, had been with the firm for more than 20 years. He set high standards for performance and expected his people to work hard to meet them, but no higher than the standards he set for himself and no harder than he himself worked. In short, he was a great leader. His sales team was in the process of negotiating a $1 billion order from one of the firm's largest customers. It was December, and a lot of pressure was on Bob to hit year-end sales objectives. The customer purchasing agent knew this and called Bob in late December with a list of conditions.

The customer purchasing agent said the company was willing to ink the deal before the end of the year if Bob agreed to a 10 percent discount. Bob thought about it and then rejected the offer. Bob believed that his company had the best product on the market and that the customer had few realistic options. Nor was he willing to give up so much profit. What happened? The customer let the year end without ordering but then unceremoniously placed the order in January. A long-term perspective is an attribute of a great leader. Missing sales goals is no fun, but like the CEO of Incredible Foods, Bob understood that margins were more important than revenues, and he knew that he could be firm in both setting and accepting terms. By doing that he earned his company $100 million in added revenue *and* profits!

Avoiding the Endowment Effect

There are many reasons why it is never easy to fire a customer or walk away from a negotiation with an existing customer. One of those reasons is what behavioral economists call the *endowment effect*.

It's a nasty trick we play on ourselves. I recently got trapped by the endowment effect. I went to the shopping mall to return a shirt. My goal was to just return the shirt and be on my way, but an expensive pair of dress slacks caught my eye and I ended up buying them. How did I get trapped? I made the mistake of entering the fitting room and trying the pants on, and then the endowment effect hijacked my brain.

The endowment effect (also known as divestiture aversion) is a hypothesis that people value a good or service more after their property right to it has been established. In other words, people place a higher value on objects they perceive they own than objects they do not. I think of it as related to loss aversion, a proposition that means that people experience the hurt of losing something much more than the gain of acquiring it. First diagnosed by Richard Thaler and Daniel Kahneman, the endowment effect stipulates that after people own something—after they have established or imagined a "property right" to the object—that something dramatically increases in subjective value.

You can see the endowment effect play out weekly during basketball season at Duke University home games in Durham, North Carolina. Duke has an undersized basketball stadium relative to other major sports franchises. The number of available tickets is much smaller than the number of people who want them. In response, the university has evolved a complicated selection process to match those tickets to the students who clamor for them. Remember, each enrolled Duke student is entitled to a ticket as a benefit. Of course, after the student receives a "free" ticket, the inexorable law of supply and demand causes the value of the ticket to rise to the market clearing price—but what is that price? Let's see how the endowment effect influences that calculation.

For each basketball game, Duke students who desire tickets put their names on a waiting list. Roughly one week before a game, fans begin pitching tents in the grass in front of Cameron Stadium. At random intervals a university official sounds an air-horn that requires that the fans check in with the basketball authority. Anyone who doesn't check in within five minutes is cut from the waiting list. At certain more desirable games, even those students who remain on the list until the bitter end aren't guaranteed a ticket, only an entry in a raffle in which they might or might not receive a ticket.

Now here's the experiment. Researchers called all the Duke students who had participated in the raffle. Posing as ticket scalpers, they asked two questions. First, they probed those who had received a ticket for the lowest amount they would sell it for. They then probed those who had *not* won a ticket for the highest amount they would pay to buy one. For the first question, the average amount that students would sell a ticket was $2,400. For the second question, the average amount that students would pay for a ticket was $170. Students who had won a ticket placed a value on the ticket roughly 14 times higher than those who had not won a ticket. How can this discrepancy be explained? This is the endowment effect in operation.

What does this have to do with fitting rooms and slacks? After I tried on the pants, I created a perception of ownership. After all, I was wearing them. The full-length mirror reflected the fact that the slacks were already mine. I admired the fit, the way the slacks made me look slimmer, how well they matched my shoes. I considered how good they would make me look when I gave a presentation the following week. Surely the $200 the slacks cost could be justified as an investment in my professional appearance. In other words, I invested a few minutes of my life imagining me owning the slacks, and after that happened, my estimation of the slacks' value increased. They suddenly began to seem like more of a bargain. Even though they were no more "mine" at that point than the mirror in the fitting room itself, I had by that point mentally endowed myself with the slacks and was loathe to "lose" something that I didn't even own. As a result, the price tag didn't seem quite so preposterous. The lesson? If you really don't want to own something, don't try it on.

In your sales work, the endowment effect can be a trap when it leads you to negotiate and secure a deal there is no chance of you actually securing. In Chapter 10, "Beware the Signs of a Losing Game," I tell the story about getting fired from a client because I recommended that it walk away from a long-established customer. Alas, my client was so invested in the endowment effect that it couldn't hear my warnings. The point I want to leave you with is simply to remember that however long you've served a customer, you do not "own" him. Every negotiation should be evaluated on its own merits and in the context of the situation as it exists in the moment.

Customer Games

Salespeople are told that listening to customers is the most important thing they can do. I agree, but there's more to listening than attending to what customers *say*. Be smart and pay attention to what customers actually *do*. Let me explain the difference. All customers say they want value above all, but sometimes the behavior of customers indicates that they really value something else even more highly. Usually, that something else is price. That doesn't make the customer undesirable or even hypocritical. It just means that there's a mixed message to decode. So which is it, value or price? The answer to that question determines the sales professional's next step. So what's a sales professional to believe?

One complicating issue of understanding what a customer wants is that you are rarely dealing with a single individual. Although some small businesses have a single purchasing manager, most companies distribute the purchasing function across departments that involve multiple people. Buying is managed in most organizations by groups of people across multiple departments who have varying levels of influence and control over the outcome. Sales professionals need to understand the buying centers to identify the decision-maker. The good news is that—all of that complexity aside—at some point a single decision-maker makes a decision. That individual is generally going to do what's in their company's best interest. This person is less likely to be deceitful and is really the one who sets the rules of the game. Also, that individual is rarely in procurement.

Whenever a disconnect exists between what a customer says and what a customer does, I give greater weight to the action. Talk, after all, is cheap. Actions usually have to be backed up with commitment, and in business the best expression of commitment is dollars. Whenever a customer points his finger and says, "Let me tell you what I value," I'm tempted to interrupt and reply, "Don't tell me what you value. Show me your department's budget, and I'll tell you what you value!" Of course, I don't do that. So that leaves the next best thing. You have to listen to the words and watch the actions to determine what kind of buying behavior the customer is displaying. Part II offers an in-depth look at those behaviors.

4

Getting the Tactics Right the First Time

This chapter examines ten tactics that can help you prepare for and win the game of procurement. In this chapter, I lay out some actionable tips and strategies to help you prepare for the different selling scenarios you will encounter. I describe these scenarios in detail in Part II, "Eight Knock-'em-Dead Scenarios for Winning the Game." The goal of this chapter is to help you start applying the tactics of pricing and selling to gain a competitive advantage against your procurement customer negotiating partner who is also, presumably, attempting to use some tactics against you. The main goal, of course, is to be able to secure the sale or the contract on a profitable basis when you have a reasonable chance of winning the business and avoiding wasting time when you can't.

This chapter presents ten specific negotiating tactics. They provide all the ammunition you need to respond to any procurement challenge. I describe each of the following tactics in detail and give examples of how you can apply them to your negotiating situation. They are as follows:

1. Qualify, qualify, qualify
2. Understand your foundation of value
3. Develop give-get options
4. Map the buying center
5. Where appropriate, build trust
6. Use the policy ploy

7. Delay, delay, delay

8. Redefine risk

9. Dealing with reverse auctions

10. Do your homework

Qualify, Qualify, Qualify

The biggest mistake salespeople and customer service people make is that they react to customer requests to do something. For example, the most costly request is the one to prepare a proposal. I'm not talking about quotes that take trivial amounts of time or effort and can be emailed to the prospect. I'm talking about those that require days, weeks, or even months to prepare. These are the proposals that take salespeople off the road. In business, time is money, and it can be used for many other valuable efforts. That time is too valuable to squander on prospects that you have zero chance of winning.

The central question for any engagement is whether the effort has a reasonable chance of securing a profitable sale. Making the request takes the customer only a few moments. It's almost a throw-away line—we've all heard it: "Sure, send me a proposal." The first tactic is *not* to prepare any proposal until you know the answers to a number of important questions. These questions all center on whether this is a legitimate request and you have a real chance of winning that business or is it part of poker playing and your price will be used to get the preferred vendor to drop their price?

In other words, you need to make a calculated, unsentimental estimation of your chances for realistically securing the business on terms that ensure you a reasonable profit. Go through the questions one by one and note the answers, but if you don't know or can't get the answers to three or more of these questions, you are almost certainly wasting your time.

Even if you agree with me, I know that rationalizing your way around this one is easy to do. I've heard all the rationalizations:

- *This client is different.*
- *I have a hunch.*
- *There's a rumor going around.*
- *I really need to close this deal.*
- *If we respond to enough RFPs, our luck is bound to change.*

Sound familiar?

It is amazing how many salespeople and professionals are willing to sink substantial amounts of time and effort in proposals when they don't know the answers to a few basic questions. Sometimes the excuse is that the proposal is due and there's no time to research the questions. Spending the time on the proposal is actually easier than going to the customer with the tough questions. The real issue is rarely one of time. The real issue is uneasiness at probing with questions that feel risky. I grant that it's not an easy process. The job of qualifying the prospect has to be done to make a determination whether responding to an RFP or a tender makes economic sense. This process can tell you whether all the subsequent work has a chance of becoming financially advantageous for the firm.

So, Tactic 1 is "qualify, qualify, qualify." Forget the selling part. Forget proposals, forget dropping off catalogs, and forget presentations and meetings. They are all premature if you haven't effectively qualified a customer opportunity. Even if you are in the middle of a proposal when you read this and you realize that you haven't qualified the opportunity, put your ego in your back pocket and drop everything. Tell the proposal team to take a break. Pick up the phone and call your contact at the customer and tell him you have more questions than answers and you need those questions answered before you can develop a formal proposal.

meeting and start qualifying the customer by asking the
estions:

- What is the process for evaluating vendors and proposals?
- What are the names and positions of everyone in the process?
- Who is the ultimate decision maker?
- What is their timeframe for evaluating vendors and finalizing the deal?
- How many other vendors are approved to supply the product or service?
- What are their names?
- Do any of those other vendors have existing relationships with the decision maker?
- Which vendor is the preferred vendor?
- What are your criteria for selection of vendors?
- Are you interested in vendors that might be able to provide more value to your firm?
- When and how do we get an opportunity to understand how we can add more value?
- Are you satisfied with your current vendor?
- If you have no prior relationship with the customer, why are they asking you to bid?
- Do budget dollars exist for the requested products and services? How much is the budget?
- What is the process to get approval to use budget dollars?

Of course, you can supplement this list with questions particular to the prospect and your product, service, or business.

Only by qualifying the buyer can you justify the expense of a proposal. If you don't get the information you ask for in an attempt to qualify the buyer, my advice is to walk away and consider yourself lucky. The one variant to this scenario is when your qualifying investigation suggests that what you are dealing with is a true price buyer—compared to other types of buyers, basic price buyers are more likely to provide answers to most of the questions you ask. After all, getting as many aggressive bids as possible is in their interest.

Whether the prospect is a good client or not, consider this: If the prospect isn't willing to answer basic questions about where you stand and you are unable to obtain the needed information in other ways, then just walk away because you're probably just wasting your time. This response is what confidence in pricing is all about.

Such confidence can pay off. The prospect might call you back and invite you to bid, and now you are in a position of strength. You can insist on the answers you need or impose such other terms as you might deem appropriate. Even if the prospect does not call, you might be content to know that you just saved a lot of time and effort that can be better focused on business that you actually have a chance to secure.

Colleagues from within your company will pressure you to respond to the proposal. At times you will not have a choice. At this point, your goal is to formulate a walkaway strategy to reset your role within the mind of the buyer. By asking tough questions about how and where your product or service is going to be used, you are sending a signal that you could very well be a good supplier. Ask technical questions that the buyer can't answer. This will worry them. They'll wonder whether the process or the specifications are right. They'll wonder whether their existing vendors really have their best interests at heart or they're just trying to sell them something. If your questions are good and tough enough, you might actually get to the decision maker. In any case, qualifying is rule number one in the selling process. Good qualification sets you up as a serious professional who is more interested in understanding the situation than trying to jam a product or service down a customer's throat—and it sends a signal that you aren't going to fall prey to those games that customers are prone to play.

Understand Your Foundation of Value

The second tactic is the holy grail of successful negotiations. After you've done all the qualifying required by the first tactic and before you get to the negotiating table, the next step is to develop an understanding of how you and your company are going to create value for the customer. Some of the basic questions to find answers for include the following:

- How are your products and services going to be used in the customer organization?
- How are your products and services different from the competitors'?
- What is that difference, if any, worth to a customer?

If you don't know your value, why should you expect your prospect to? If you can't communicate the real and tangible value you can deliver, no price exists that is going to be low enough to satisfy your prospect. However, if you know, for example, that your system or service is going to provide an additional $1 million in cost reductions and subsequent profits for a customer, you have real power. If a customer is trying to get you to drop your price from $50,000 to $49,000, then using your understanding of the value you add, not only to resist the discounting but also to perhaps argue for an increase in price, is easy.

Knowing your value puts your price in perspective. Knowing your value and being able to express it in terms of the prospect's business helps defend your price. Sometimes this information helps correct pricing mistakes. You are making a price mistake if you are charging $2 million for a solution that yields just $1 million in benefits. Clear financial value to the customers puts pricing into perspective. The more deeply you understand how your company arrived at the price, the better you can defend it. The point is that if you know your value is high and your price is fair given that value, it should make you willing to fight for your price rather than rolling over and discounting to make the procurement people happy. The value becomes the foundation of good pricing and good negotiations.

Where and how do you get the information to assess value? You ask your customers simple, open-ended questions that focus on how they operate and how they could use your equipment or services. How would your solution make a difference to them? How would this solution set you apart from your competitors, and what is that worth to you? The information will help you build a better calculation on value, and it will be much more credible in the actual selling and negotiating situation. This is a listening event with your client, which means no selling, no problem-solving, just active listening. Later on you can come back with a solution based on the needs they described. Here are a few simple elements of how you do that.

- **Apply the KISS principle (Keep It Simple, Stupid):** Keep your questions and your analysis simple. Clarity is what you are seeking. The easiest thing to do is lose sight of the main goal, which is to persuade the prospect that you have the most cost-effective solution. I once worked with a medical devices company and was astounded to see that it submitted a proposal that calculated the cost of the cotton swabs that would be required to maintain the device. However, the proposal failed to underscore a very specific way that the device would add measurable strategic value to the customer's organization. The vendor sales team got so involved in figuring out the minute details that it missed several of the bigger drivers of value for the hospitals. Focus on finding all sources of value and understand how the important attributes operate for a customer and how you impact that operation, and by all means, don't be afraid to keep it simple.

- **Focus on costs *and* profits:** Much value work focuses on cost reductions. Cost reductions are important, but they are often less than half the story. Some years ago IT outsourcing firms focused their value propositions on cost savings. Every year the customer expects more savings, efficiency, and a greater discount from this model. This is a spiral effect that is hard to break. Think about how your products and services will help a customer sell more, too—that's often a bigger number than the cost reductions, and that relative importance should be reflected in the proposal. Everyone wants incremental revenue, but not everyone recognizes the opportunity costs of missing business. Our client from the earlier example was so focused on cotton swabs that he missed the fact that the new product had several special features that would help the customer sell more services that were quite profitable due to that customer's particular reimbursement schedule.

- **Be conservative:** Use customers' estimates of how they will achieve value. Let them give you current efficiencies and operating values. If they are smart, they will be conservative. You should be, too. If you have to make estimates, stay conservative; make them at the low end of the range. Doing so builds your credibility with the customer and increases the likelihood that the customer, though maybe not procurement, will believe your value estimates.

- **Get to a number with a dollar sign:** In the end, your value analysis should provide your customer with a number—that is, a number with a dollar sign. Almost all companies recognize the importance of value. They train their salespeople to use the word *value*, but without the financial return it is all rhetoric, which is useless to a customer. Eventually, you have to come to a number. My advice is to get to it sooner rather than later. Recognize that it takes more than value for relationship and even value buyers. Trust is a key driver of some customer decisions. If you don't develop trust, all the value in the world won't help. Through all this discussion of dealing with procurement, the value you provide and the trust that a decision maker has in you and your firm is what provides you with the power and leverage in tough negotiations. Without it, you will always be a victim of the procurement pricing buzz saw.

Companies often fail to equip salespeople with an effective understanding of how their organizations create value. Offering trade-offs—that is, offers with different levels of value, or a portfolio—can help. Without an understanding of value or the trade-offs that can be made, nickel and dime negotiations are inevitable. The purpose of this second tactic, understanding your foundation of value, is to give salespeople and managers an understanding of the context of the price negotiations—how they fit in to the bigger picture of value. Procurement managers will often tell you that all vendors are the same, but that is rarely true. To play the sales game, you must understand the value of your product and service and its relevance in the decision process.

Develop Give-Get Options

A give-get is a simple sales tactic that is invoked when a client demands a price discount. The give-get response says to the customer, "You want to get a price discount? No problem, but you'll have to give up something of value at the same time." You get something, you give something. Give-get is a tactic that salespeople use to send the message that they are willing to negotiate to provide lower prices, but they are confident enough to connect the discount with changes in value as well. It is a way of being both responsive and controlling. Give-get is the most elemental tactic in bluffing out the poker-playing procurement people.

When a salesperson drops price in a negotiation, the buyer knows that the game is on. After you start agreeing to discount, the customer has every incentive to continue negotiating to see how low you are willing to go. The give-get tactic is a way to stop that downward cycle of price discounts in a negotiation. Sure, a good procurement person is going to sweep the first offer off the table, so have back-up give-gets to use when she does that. You might need to be creative in coming up with ways to justify discounts with scope changes, product unbundling, even things such as turnaround time. Sometimes the words you use have great import. Never use the term *discount*—just "restructure" the plan.

I often use this tactic in my business when clients ask me to reduce prices after we have agreed on a fee. I am okay with doing so because the structure of our business is such that I can reduce the work effort or scope at the same level our clients reduce their spend. When customers give less money, they get less value. We are able to protect our margins precisely because we have designed how we do business with give-get options in mind.

To make give-get options real, a seller's offerings must be able to be seamlessly unbundled in response to demands for pricing concessions. In the most basic cases, salespeople present customers with two choices: a higher-price, full service offering and a low-price, bare-bones offering. The customer gets to choose. Typically, the unbundling of services and features is taken on a case-by-case basis. The important thing to remember is to structure the offering in a way that you can make trade-offs when procurement asks for a discount. With this leverage, you can give them the requested discount, but they pay a price in terms of receiving lower value. In my experience, many customers back off the discount-focused negotiation when they realize that they will also receive less value.

To create give-get offerings, keep the following pricing guidelines in mind:

- Match offerings with the value needs of target customers. Remember, not all customers want value, let alone the top tier of the offering.
- Offer lower-value flanking products that appeal to price-sensitive customers.

- Offer high-value bundles of products and services that appeal to customers that are able and willing to pay for them.

- Build strong fences protecting high- from low-value offerings to prevent customers from negotiating for high-value offerings at low prices.

- Arm sales with well-defined ways to alter the offering value and prices by adding or removing specific features.

The alternatives referred to in the preceding bullet can be based solely on product features, the services that get wrapped around the products or services alone. The important thing is that they have some value for the client. Another aspect of value can be based on immediate access to goods and/or services. This is a terrific way to get the customer to focus on the value of time. Quote a low price for a four-week lead time and a high price for immediate access; you'll find out quickly who the poker players are. The price could be a function of product or software features, or it could be based on the availability of expert people in your firm who will be providing the service.

Consider a company whose specialty is building large commercial projects. Some of its project managers are first-class—expert at getting the project done on time to specific customer specifications. There are others who are learning the craft and are somewhat less experienced. The company has learned to do two things to better play the procurement game. One is that it has established a tiered pricing structure. It charges $600 for the top-level project managers and $300 for the project managers on the next tier. Now customers can select what level of engagement they prefer. Another tactic is that the company has announced an internal policy that its top-level project managers are available only for the most profitable projects.

These options work best if they are coordinated with the product and service strategy of the organization. Accordingly, give-get (sometimes called flanking) product strategies require some time and resources to develop properly, but they are the most concrete elements to be used in price negotiations by salespeople. When they are concrete and part of the intentional strategy, salespeople can be trained on their use and subsequently make trade-offs with them more effectively.

Sellers will sometimes avoid developing flanking offerings because of the complexity it adds to their business operations. That give-get options create more complexity for the organization is accurate, but that cost is often small compared to the financial and negotiating leverage that a salesperson gets by having those extra products in the line. That's because if a low-value offering isn't available, the only change you can make in a negotiation is price—and price in most negotiations goes in only one direction—and it isn't up.

After you start down the slippery slope of discounting, stopping is quite difficult, but having a lower value offering gives you an alternative to present to customers that helps change the discussion from exclusively price to one of value. Changes in value help customers discriminate higher and lower prices and why they are different.

Several years ago, a senior executive challenged my push to add additional products to his offering a portfolio. When I asked him why—he indicated that it added costs to the operation. When I asked him how much, he thought for a moment, made a few calculations on the whiteboard in his office, and said, "$18,000." I then spent a few minutes at the whiteboard and did some calculations of my own. I showed him how much extra revenue the extra give-get products would generate and the incremental profit that would fall to the bottom line. The incremental profits exceeded the incremental costs by a ratio of more than a hundred to one. The executive swallowed hard and retracted his challenge to the give-get strategy.

On the other hand, product proliferation imposes its own disadvantages. The added complexity needs to be considered. The law of diminishing returns always operates. It's like the number of gears on a bicycle. If three speeds are okay, 10 speeds are good, and 18 speeds are even better, then maybe 50 gears would be better still. The problem is that we know by experience that the added cost, complexity, and additional weight of those extra speeds do not justify any small incremental advantage. It's the same thing with the number of give-get offerings. As in all things, a fine balance between too few and too many product offerings must be maintained. If salespeople do not have enough variables or elements they can negotiate with, they will be at a disadvantage against salespeople with a greater range of negotiating options, but if they offer too many features and price combinations, customers will be confused, and the pricing complexity becomes too burdensome for the company to manage. A good give-get balance protects the profits of high-value products because salespeople can offer the lower-value version rather than reducing the price of the high-value products. Meanwhile, the lower-value product, if sold properly, can become a fighting brand to compete with lower-value competitors. Most importantly, the right balance gives salespeople the optimum range of products with which to negotiate. During presentations, I often get a question about how to calibrate that balance. Some salespeople argue that the more product offerings they have to work with, the more aggressively they can compete. So which is it, optimum or maximum? I reply by noting that optimum human body temperature is 98.6 degrees Fahrenheit. Maximum body temperature will drop you every time.

A properly executed give-get strategy is comprised of four elements, as discussed in the following sections.

Try Give-Get Bluffs

Creative salespeople and executives can often make up their own strategies on the fly. I'm thinking of a senior sales executive who was in an intense price negotiation with a domestic automobile manufacturer. The car company's procurement officer demanded a price discount. The sales manager was ready. He had just finished preparing the value exercise described in the "Understand the Foundation of Value" section of this chapter. The analysis identified his particular product as a critical component in the exhaust emissions system of the car company's most profitable line of vehicles. Because he had done his homework, the sales manager replied that he could meet the price discount demand by delivering a planned cost-reduced product. The sales manager made sure the procurement agent understood that this lower-cost product could not be made to the critical specifications required by the car company and delivered by the existing product. The procurement person quickly backed off of his negotiating position and decided to continue his purchase of the higher-priced product. He did so because he knew it was critical to the mission. The sales manager displayed confidence. He used an effective give-get bluff to show the real value of the higher priced product. Because he bluffed well, he won the pot—higher prices and more profits for the firm. Such outcomes are possible in every industry, including the tough negotiating world of the automotive supply business.

Provide Value-Added Services

Services of all varieties can be an effective facilitator for the give-get option. Those services can be delivered with or wrapped around a product, even a commodity product. The simpler and more valuable the service, the more appropriate it is to serve as a give-get offering. Here's a story that illustrates what I mean by *simple*. The selling company is a commodity building products business, and the commodity product is undifferentiated except by price from what a number of competitors offered. To complicate matters, the competitors all use price discounting aggressively to win. This scenario is normally a disaster for commodity product pricing, but the seller listened to its customers carefully and determined a service offering that could give them a competitive advantage. The seller learned that what the customers valued most—perhaps more than the price of the product itself—was getting their trucks through the pick-up facility as quickly as possible. With the price of gasoline and rising costs of transportation, getting those trucks loaded up and on the road quickly represented real savings. The seller next developed a give-get offering that gave its customers two tiers of service. The first was basic service for the lowest possible cost. The second was similar to the priority boarding line at the airport for the travelers with "Gold" status. If the customer paid a little more, its trucks went to the front of the line, and the loading was expedited. If a customer wanted the lowest possible price, no problem, but its trucks had longer waits.

Value-added services provide perhaps the best opportunity for give-get options in selling and negotiating. They have to be well thought out and especially well executed. Discipline in execution is mandatory. If customers learn that by calling and complaining they can get to the front of the line without paying the higher price, the tactic falls apart. With logic in establishing the proper service structure and discipline in its execution, even commodity suppliers are able to improve the results in pricing, negotiating, and profits.

Use the Concepts of Scarcity and Availability

There's an old joke about two small pickle vendors doing business on the lower east side of New York City at the beginning of the twentieth century. A man walks into Joe's Pickles and inquires about prices. "Pickles are two for a nickel," Joe responds. The man says, "But for a nickel I can get three pickles at Sam's!" Joe responds, "So, buy your pickles at Sam's." The customer looks at his feet and says, "Sam is out of pickles today." Joe says, "Yes, well, when I'm out of pickles, they're also three for a nickel."

Scarcity imposes its own rules. I remember a company that was selling a commodity electronic product that suddenly found itself in short supply. The company immediately introduced another product with similar performance as the scarce product, in stock at a 60 percent price premium. Customers didn't complain about the price—they were just glad to get access to the product. This company used availability as a value differentiator to a commodity product and charged for it. This gave salespeople good leverage and complete confidence in negotiations. If the customer wanted the lower price of the scarce item, the company would be happy to take his order. The customer would just have to wait an unknown number of weeks until the product supply chain could be replenished. Meanwhile, if they wanted immediate delivery, they must agree to the premium price.

Provide Choices

Give-get options allow value and relationship customers choices to configure the best value for their specific situations. I sometimes talk to salespeople who propose a single option because they think giving customers choices complicates the selling process. It might, but when things get complex is when the salesperson earns his or her commission: by taking on complexity to better solve a problem for the customer. In some cases, of course, a single option might be so finely tuned and appropriate that different customers are well-served, but in most cases, customers are better served when treated as individuals with differing needs. Importantly, in a company that has a portfolio of offerings, or tiers of low- to high-value offerings, salespeople can more easily suggest choices. Customers can decide whether they want to pay for the higher value choice and they can more easily discriminate the differences.

Consider the different buying behaviors exhibited by customers that we discuss in the next four chapters. Price buyers neither want nor need choice. Relationship buyers generally have considered the alternatives and settled on one vendor. A give-get strategy at this point allows the salesperson to say, "We believe the higher-value option is best for you, but if you are more concerned about costs at this point, then the lower-priced option will work with some limitations." Of course, the salesperson then has to be scrupulous in defining those limitations. Doing so builds credibility and trust in the salesperson. For value buyers, choice says that you have looked at the alternatives and have a high-value and a low-value alternative. Because value buyers generally tend to purchase the higher value, chances are they will go with the high-value option and they will appreciate that the salesperson didn't attempt to sell a low-value option that might not have met their requirements. The key, though, is to offer them choices.

Where the give-get option works best, and is needed most, is in responding to the poker player customer. Poker players' basic premise is that they can get the salesperson to deliver a high-value offering for a lower price. They generally do that by either saying that their budget has been cut or that another supplier has quoted a lower price. They expect the high-value offer at the low-value offer price. Most poker players don't worry about justifying their negotiating stance. They offer it as an ultimatum. Whatever the justification or lack of one, the give-get strategy enables the salesperson to match the lower price by offering a flanking product that protects the price of the higher-value product. Of course, the customer will then insist that the lower-priced product won't do. They must have the higher-priced product at the lower price. This is where the salesperson, remembering that he or she represents the buyer's preferred vendor, gets to call their bluff.

Map the Buying Center

Purchasing in organizations is rarely done solely by an individual. Instead it is done by a group of individuals who fulfill various roles and use different criteria with different levels of involvement. The job of the salesperson preparing for either a sale or a negotiation is to understand who is in the buying center, what role they play, what buyer behavior they exhibit, and what is important to them in evaluating various vendors.

This information is important because if a salesperson relies on an internal contact or informant at the client, he will only get part of the picture. A procurement person is going to have different evaluation criteria, usually focused only on price, and she is going to try to control the game to favor what's important to her rather than what's important to other people in the buying center.

Procurement people have also been known to distort the facts and lie about a vendor's position in the process. They do this so they control the game and get the best deal for their organization—usually high value at a low price. We've already discussed some of their tricks in the game, but the point here is that salespeople who only speak with procurement people are getting a skewed idea of the game they need to play.

Only when salespeople understand who else is in the process and what is important to those people can they get a true picture of not only the game but their position in that game as well.

To succeed in their bluffing game, procurement people need to limit your access to their colleagues. That is the gatekeeper role. They do that for a number of reasons, including the following:

- So they can dictate the rules of the game
- So you don't "disturb" their colleagues and end up with a contact, maybe a decision maker who you can go meet with directly
- So they make sure that the deal is done at the best possible terms for their firm without any possibility of your obtaining information about your real value and position that could make you a stronger negotiator

The job of the salesperson is to understand the position at the table that the procurement person is playing and get to other members of the buying center who are involved with the process to determine what is really going on—what other vendors are involved, how they are viewed, and what is valuable to the customer organization.

Sometimes technical support people in the selling organization can be helpful in that process. We were involved with one negotiation where the procurement person was playing a strong gatekeeping role and limiting access to the rest of the team. The salesperson had his technical person visit with the client's technical team, and he was able to confirm that their position was as the preferred vendor. That information helped us craft a higher-priced strategy based on the value we knew we had. The negotiations with the poker-playing procurement person were long and arduous, but they eventually closed a very large and profitable deal.

Identifying the decision maker is perhaps the most difficult part of this tactic because he or she is often protected and hidden by the gatekeeper. The fact that you don't know or aren't able to meet with the decision maker is typically a dangerous sign—especially in the professional services business where senior executives often have longstanding relationships with providers. If you don't have the relationship, you are in a weak position in the decision process—We'll talk about why this is important in the following chapters. But remember that if you don't have the right relationship, you probably aren't going to get the business. Revisit Tactic 1 and ask the hard qualifying questions that point to the value you bring. Asking them are enough to rattle the procurement person and get you to the decision maker or other members of their buying center to have value- or relationship-oriented discussions. Start with this qualifying question: Who is the decision maker and what is the nature of their relationships with other vendors in this purchase? No answer is a complete answer. If the answer is negative or you don't have an answer, the conclusion is that you simply don't have the right relationship to win this one.

Understanding the buying center is a critical tactic to prepare for the negotiation. It advises a salesperson on his position in the process, what he has to do in order to win the order, and the likelihood that he can even do that.

e Appropriate, Build Trust

The most basic lubricant to both relationship and value buyers is trust. These buyers, more than price buyers, need to have trust in their supplier or vendor. Trust is a big subject, and surveying the ways vendors gain and lose trust is beyond the scope of this book. In Stephen Covey's new book, *The SPEED of Trust: The One Thing that Changes Everything*, the author of *The Seven Habits of Highly Successful Leaders* defines trust as a combination of character (who you are) and competence (your strengths and the results you produce). Trust, according to Covey, is a measurable, definable component of leadership success and influence.

When the trust between the customer and vendor is compromised, the results are immediately obvious and not in a way that benefits either party. Low trust imposes a cost on performance at every level. The following characteristics of low-trust relationships impose extraneous friction on the partnership that high-trust relationships avoid:

- Facts are manipulated or distorted.
- Information and knowledge are withheld and hoarded.
- Mistakes are covered up or covered over.
- Most people are involved in a blame game, badmouthing others.
- Numerous "meetings after the meetings" occur.
- People tend to overpromise and underdeliver.
- A lot of violated expectations occur, for which people make many excuses.
- People pretend bad things aren't happening or are in denial. The net result is that problems and subsequent costs go up.

When customers have trust in a vendor, the trust serves as a performance multiplier that has a measurable value in the negotiations. When trust goes up, costs go down, producing what I call a "trust dividend." This should not be surprising. In low-trust environments, negotiating partners have to spend time and money on processes designed to offer verification and build confidence. Transactions without such overhead naturally proceed quicker and less expensively. The research is clear—organizations with high trust outperform organizations with low trust by nearly three times (WorkUSA® Study, Watson Wyatt 2002).

Trust in the seller is the key distinguishing factor between price and non-price buying behavior. If a vendor is going to be successful in going after relationship- or value-oriented clients, it must develop a culture that encourages managers and salespeople to exhibit the cultural behaviors that promote trust. Some of these behaviors include the following:

- Supplying promised quality
- Responsive customer service
- Lack of high-pressure selling tactics
- Asks about and listens to customer problems
- Company reliability and on-time delivery
- Salesperson reliability—confidence that the salesperson can deliver on promises

Covey lists the following characteristics as elements of a high-trust relationship between organizations and their vendors:

- There is a low customer/vendor churn rate.
- Customer and supplier relationships last longer.
- Positive reputation and brand equity grows in the marketplace.
- Information is shared openly.
- Mistakes are tolerated and encouraged as a way of learning.
- Employees talk straight and confront real issues.
- Few "meetings after the meetings" occur.
- Transparency is a practiced value.

- People are candid and authentic.
- A high degree of accountability exists.

If you are truly dealing with a value or a relationship buyer, then trust is an important determinant of their doing business with you. Building trust takes time and patience, and frankly, you'll have some customers who won't care about it. These are the price buyers.

Use the Policy Ploy

The policy ploy is a tactic whereby the salesperson responds to a demand for a discount or other concession by stating, "I'm sorry, company policy prohibits me from doing that." By definition, a *policy* is a decision made in advance. In truth there's nothing final about any decision, but the word *policy* has an attractive quality of non-negotiability. The policy ploy tactic short-circuits the customer's call for new contract terms by declaring that the requested course of action is prohibited by policy. In other words, the policy ploy is a tactic to pass the buck to a higher authority, often a higher authority that is made up on the spot.

In reality, a policy is just a decision made in advance, whether it was decided by the board of directors six months ago or decided by the salesperson six seconds ago. There's something about invoking policy that often preempts the request.

We were in a recent deal when suddenly procurement jumped in and took over the negotiation. They systematically went through our statement of work, dropped the price, and inserted a long list of terms and conditions. We dealt with the price and the terms and conditions, but one particular sticking point on risk sharing would have cost us a big discount and put a large portion of the project at risk. That's when I invoked the policy ploy, which stopped the procurement person in her tracks and gave me control of the process.

Delay, Delay, Delay

One of the greatest tools that procurement people use against their vendors is time. Effective procurement people know that the salespeople can be under intense pressure to close the deal, especially at the end of the quarter. Often that pressure is imposed from management. Sometimes, the pressure is self-imposed, either by the desire on the part of a salesperson for more income or to garner the annual prize for best sales performance (the winner goes on a two-week trip to Hawaii, second place gets the steak knives). In any case, procurement people know that salespeople with quotas believe that time is their enemy.

The delay tactic is when time is being used against a salesperson. He must recognize that in many cases, when time is used against him, the procurement person is sweating over whether the tactic is going to work. Does this surprise you? It happens! In fact, I argue that time is neutral. It can hurt the customer as much as it can hurt the salesperson. Sometimes more. After all, the procurement person reports to a senior executive who has intense pressure to manage a product pipeline and keep it filled. The job of the procurement person depends on maintaining that supply.

When I attended training for advanced procurement techniques, the other attendees were procurement professionals with 15 to 20 years of experience. We talked about the time delay tactic, and all of them, even the instructor, had stories about how they had used it and sweated whether the supplier was going to fall for the trick. Suppliers usually caved at the last moment, making the tactic very successful for the procurement side.

When salespeople recognize the delay tactic, the trick is to use it against the procurement people. If they delay, you delay more. If they want to schedule a meeting in a week, you delay it for two weeks. If they say they'll call you back in a week, don't follow up for two weeks. Yes, that's right. Just wait. I can feel you cringing at this advice. You want to rush to close the deal. That's the nature of the salesperson, and procurement knows it! However, if you can control this one attitude, you'll be much more successful in closing the deal. Poker-playing procurement people will ask for deep discounts and then slow down or even shut down negotiations. Procurement hopes that the salespeople will cave in the face of these delays and persuade their superiors to agree to the demands.

Not all such delays are gambits or bluffs. Sometimes delays are introduced by legitimate extenuating circumstances such as the departure of a procurement person or other changes in the management structure of the customer, but usually the customer will be more or less transparent about such circumstances. If no specific reasons are given or emerge to explain a delay, you can safely bet that the delay is intentional, part of the procurement playbook to use against suppliers. So salespeople need to recognize the tactic and use it back— procurement people won't expect it and will be put off balance when it is used against them. I know of a CEO of a software company who is really patient and willing to wait out procurement. He expects his salespeople to push for the close, but if procurement gets involved and begins delaying the process and bringing in other vendors to try to drive their price down, he gets involved and slows down his team. He is quite willing to wait out procurement, and he is very successful.

Recently, a customer attempted to use the delay tactic against me. I knew that we were the chosen firm. I had confidence that other firms were no longer under consideration. I was anticipating receipt of the agreement that we had negotiated so we could get to work. All of a sudden, a procurement official got involved and imposed three new conditions that had the effect of reducing the agreed-upon fee by a third. I don't mind telling you I got very angry. Luckily, I followed my own advice and did an extra workout to relieve the emotion. It's frustrating, but I remembered my own advice: Never, ever negotiate out of emotion.

So what was my response? I decided to delay. The procurement person requested a meeting. I delayed it for a week. I told them that my team needed more time to review the additional terms that the procurement official had added. Based on my understanding of the client's situation, I knew there was internal time pressure. I contemplated that my delaying tactics put the client in a tighter bind than they perceived their delaying tactics placed me. The client's management team pressured for a resolution to the negotiation so my company could do a job that is central to their success. Finally, we got the agreement. It was on our original terms!

Redefine Risk

When customers buy from vendors, there are instances that involve greater levels of risk. The risk could be around product failure, delayed delivery, systems problems, and so on. All services have inherent risk in performance—the list is probably endless. The risk of non- or underperformance in a purchasing agreement is something that procurement people are trying to control. There are two types of risk to think about. The first is performance risk. From a performance perspective, the procurement people are correct in trying to get vendors to step up and agree to meet some level of performance criteria in the contract. This could be in terms of system uptime, meantime between failures, response time for a service contract, or a specific outcome in a professional service-level agreement (SLA).

The second type to consider is how risk is used by procurement people to put downward pressure on prices. This is a major element in contract negotiations for many process systems and high-value services so the final tactic is to discuss is how risk associated with price reductions creep into contract discussions and how we should respond. What they are trying to do is to get you to accept performance risk in your contract. Performance risk varies on the type of work being done or equipment being supplied. Risk in this case is that performance is going to be what you have said it will be during the selling process.

The first thing to remember is that if you are down to a serious discussion of guaranteeing performance, you are a preferred vendor. Be careful here because at times a client will ask whether you are willing to guarantee a performance factor you've just presented. If your answer is anything but "absolutely," you are sending a signal that you can't be trusted. You should be willing to guarantee how you say you are going to perform. Doing so shows both trustworthiness and confidence. If you *do* guarantee something, recognize that a guarantee represents high value and must be associated with a higher price.

When procurement gets involved with the contract negotiations, they will often try to put a percentage of the overall fee "at risk." They want you to have "some skin in the game." You get a final payment if you live up to your guarantees. They do that with "strategic partners." If you find yourself starting to panic, that is their intent. They feel that it is a great way to get discounts along the way. How you react in risk-based discussions is important, and that reaction has to be real—none of it can be a bluff. You have to "love" risk-based contracts. Why? The answer is because you are so confident in the ability of your company to perform and your company can make more money.

When you find yourself in a discussion with procurement where they want you to take some risk, point out that the correct term is "risk-reward." That is, if you are putting a portion of the contract at risk or under some level of performance terms, the give-get for doing that is to participate in the rewards or value that adopting your product or service is going to bring to your customer. That's another reason why Tactic 2 (understand the foundation of value) is so important. If procurement has decided to change the game, you take it up a level. You should have already defined the value you are bringing to the game; just pick a "fair" incremental percentage of that reward beyond the proposed price for the work. Suddenly, the tables are turned on procurement when they start negotiating with you based on the value you are going to bring to the customer—a game that favors you.

I recall an incident where a procurement person demanded a risk adjustment to a contract we were negotiating. He made several mistakes along the way. For one thing, because the original contract was sizable, he started by arbitrarily reducing the fee by 35 percent. Not content with this, the procurement person then insisted that 30 percent of his new arbitrary fee was "at risk." In other words, he wanted to retain 30 percent of the fee until the project met some performance milestones, to be later identified. He was trying to see what he could get away with.

After a suitable cooling-off period on my part, the first thing I did was to separate the two issues so they didn't get confused. I said that if he wanted the price to be 35 percent lower, I would be happy to rescope the work effort and offer him a revised statement of work. On the risk issue, I replied that we appreciated the opportunity to be accountable for any risk for which we were responsible, but the appropriate standard is not just risk, but risk-reward. In other words, I was prepared to take the hit for any downside we were responsible for but only if we also shared in the upside. Fair is fair. If the customer wanted us to take on some of the project risk, we would also share in the reward. He agreed.

I responded that I would be delighted to split the reward portion with them but would only need to do that in the first year. The procurement person immediately tried to negotiate my share of the projected reward to 30 percent from the assumed 50 percent share. I agreed. Why? Because I had done my homework. I calculated that the expected result of the work would exceed $8 million in the first year. And it was a conservative estimate—the real value was going to be much higher. I work hard to pin down the value a client will get from our work. I further said that my company's policy limited the amount of a project that could be put at risk to a maximum of 20 percent of the fee. By the way, I made up the policy on the fly just before the meeting. He agreed. By refocusing the risk portion of the negotiations to risk/reward, I changed the rules of the game and actually undermined the procurement person's negotiating leverage in the process.

Here's how I knew we had undermined the credibility of the procurement function. Several weeks later, the key decision maker at the customer phoned me. The executive expressed concern about the terms of the contract. I pointed out that the contract was actually not in the customer's best interest. We would help them make so much money they would have to cut us a big check at the end of the project as our share of the reward. I said I'd be happy to go back to the original terms of the contract we negotiated before procurement got involved. Subsequently, we signed the contract on mutually agreeable terms, we performed as promised, and we never heard from that procurement executive again.

When customers trot out the issue of risk, it's often another attempt to get suppliers to accept lower prices and hold back some of their fee. This tactic represents a big red flag to suppliers, but it is also an indicator to push back and redefine "risk" to "risk-reward." Redefining the issue as risk-reward indicates that you are willing to take on some risk if the customer experiences specified losses due to your performance, but only to the extent that you participate in reward if the customer experiences specified gains.

Dealing with Reverse Auctions

Good procurement people know that there is no better way to rattle valued suppliers than to put them through a reverse auction. They use cool software that categorizes the players as A, B, C, and so on. You know you are B, but you don't know the identities of anyone else. You know that there is one other vendor that is valued, so the other vendor is probably a second-tier vendor who was added into the mix to drive your price down. They give you a day, several days, or a week. You sit there with your team watching the price drop. You have your finance guy in the room, maybe even your CFO to help in the cost recalculations all to help determine how many costs you can take off the plate to justify the price that inevitably slips down below the profit point of all reason.

The process is designed to be the ultimate poker game: guts poker with no opportunity to bluff. At least *you* have no opportunity to bluff. They are bluffing (and laughing) all the way to the bank. I want you to think about that. Forget the office you and your team are sitting in for a moment and think about the office they are sitting in. Think about the procurement person with the team of users and real buyers who have been your loyal customers for the past bunch of years. Think about how they watch the prices drop to the point of financial oblivion. Think about the procurement people laughing with glee as they watch the price drop. Hear them say, "See, I told you so. I told you those guys were screwing us all these years." Do you have the picture now? Are you a little angry? Good. That's right where I want you. I want you a little angry before you go into one of those reverse auctions. That way you will end up doing your homework before you go into the lunacy of the game.

What should you do if a client asks you to participate in a reverse auction? Easy—you assess their likely behavior and your position. If they are purchasing a true commodity, there are a bunch of equal vendors, and you already know how to play the Penny Pincher game. (See Chapter 5, "Negotiating with Price Buyers.) You keep your costs to the bare bones. You don't add any non-valued services, and you know what your walk away price is. If the client is truly a value buyer and has sucked two other vendors into playing the game, and you are all Crafty Outsiders (see Chapter 7, "Negotiating with Value Buyers), then you had better hope they/you don't do anything stupid with price. Remember, though, if you have a desperate competitor or a competitor that doesn't have a good control system around price, you are already in trouble. You need to decide if you can win the business with a profitable price—you probably can't!

However, if you don't fit into either the Penny Pincher or Crafty Outsider situation, then you are filling only one of two others possible—the Rabbit or the Advantaged Player. (See Chapter 8, "Negotiating with Poker Players.") If you are the Rabbit—you know what to do—stop playing the game and don't agree to play in the first place. What else can you do if you are asked to be the Rabbit? Use the request as an opportunity to ask a whole series of qualifying questions to determine the real value needs of the customer and the decision process and structure. Just don't play the auction game. If you are the Advantaged Player, then recognize that if you play the game as they have defined it, you are both validating the process and telling the other members of the buying center that you have been screwing them in the past.

What should you do? You should think about not playing. Believe it or not, I've been watching companies get sucked into reverse auctions for more than 20 years. My advice is the same now as it was then—don't play. When I have a reverse auction thrust on me, I say I'm not interested. In some of those cases the result was that the reverse auction was withdrawn. The customer wised up and realized that its trusted supplier wasn't going to play the game.

Some vendors think that dropping the price a little to participate in a reverse auction sometimes makes sense. This thinking makes me cringe. Anything you do to validate the process is eventually going to work against you. You might try to justify it by saying you are only going to give a little discount—but that's just the validation customers are looking for. It only encourages clients to have more reverse auctions. Here's what I recommend instead: Have a frank dialogue with your client about how you are perfectly willing to discuss ways to bring prices down using give-gets, but the reverse auction is just going to add to your costs, which means a possible price hike.

Do Your Homework

Effective procurement people know a lot about their preferred vendor partners. They have studied their income statements, balance sheets, cash flow, and other corporate reports. They know what the vendor does well, what it doesn't do well, and their revenue, growth, and profit margins. Salespeople need to be equally up to speed on the strategy, financial strength, and the performance of their company and the prospect if they want to compete on a level playing field. This homework is more than doing the other steps we've discussed— applying the buying center, the foundation of value, and the qualifying questions tactics. This is about digging on the Internet about the company they are selling to, the competitors, and the industry. This is about reading the annual reports and 10-Ks. It's about reading the analysts' reports that might note changes or concerns in the industry or the company.

I remember one prospect I was able to convert to a client when I looked at how their income statement was behaving on a year-to-year basis. I realized that when the raw materials prices were going down, they were making a lot of money. I predicted the prospect was concerned that when the raw material prices were going up, it wouldn't know what to do. I was right, and that concern became one of the value drivers that caused the client to decide to select us and go ahead with the project. Bottom line: Do your homework.

These are ten good tactics to help salespeople prepare and play the great game of procurement. None are difficult to master, but all require some level of confidence and the occasional bluff to pull off effectively. Confidence and bluffing are two key elements of effective negotiations. Combine confidence with legwork, advanced preparation, and discipline, and you will be in a superior negotiating position. Plan to practice the tactics ahead of time. To win at the great game of procurement, get the job done before you reach the negotiating table.

Part II

Eight Knock-'em-Dead Scenarios
for Winning the Game

Part II describes eight step-by-step negotiating scenarios using winning responses for each of the four buyer types. To summarize, the four buyer types are

- **Price buyers:** These customers want to buy products and services only at the lowest possible price. They don't care about value, differentiation, or relationships.

- **Relationship buyers:** These customers want to trust and have dependable relationships with their suppliers and expect that supplier to take good care of them.

- **Value buyers:** These customers tend to be sophisticated buyers who understand value and want suppliers to be able to provide the most value in their relationship.

- **Poker Player buyers:** These are relationship or value buyers who have learned that if they act like a price buyer, they can get high value for low prices.

Each buyer behavior is associated with a specific set of agendas requiring a different offering, pricing, and selling approach. Determining the behavior of procurement or economic buyers can be difficult, especially with all the tactics they have developed to shield their true needs under the cloak of the price buyer. To have sales success, sales professionals must be able to recognize the behaviors to craft the right response in each sales situation.

Seller's Position

After salespeople have identified which of the four buying behaviors are exhibited by the customer, their next step is to understand what their position is relative to those behaviors. The possibilities are actually limited. Either they are in a relationship with the decision maker or they aren't. Everything else is secondary. The single biggest predictor of whether a salesperson will get the sale is whether or not he has a relationship with the decision maker. Many ways exist for measuring whether two people have a relationship, but in this case, the test is rather simple: Have the salesperson and buyer done satisfactory business together in the past, or does the salesperson have an introduction from a trusted intermediary inside or outside the buying firm so that he can effectively qualify how the decision will really be made? The qualifying questions, discussed in Chapter 4, "Getting the Tactics Right the First Time," are designed to accomplish two things—to determine the game and get you to the decision maker.

Without this condition existing, the answer, regrettably, is no; no relationship exists. In such cases, the prospective sale becomes much, much less likely. Can a sale be made without a pre-existing relationship between the buyer and the salesperson? Sure, it's possible. It always helps if the salesperson can demonstrate an understanding of the buyer's business. Such an understanding might get the salesperson an audience, and that audience might lead to a relationship, but it's not easy. A salesperson needs to be able to evaluate a decision maker's specific selection criteria, and generally the only way to do that is with a direct meeting.

Understanding the salesperson's relationship in the context of the buyer's behavior is important because that overlay dictates a total of eight possible scenarios. Each of these eight scenarios, in turn, predicts the specific tactics that a customer will employ and dictates the particular countertactics with which the salesperson will respond. Often these tactics are quite subtle in their operation, but paying attention to the differences is important if salespeople are going to play the game well and get the best outcome for their organizations. To get the best handle on these scenarios, you must attend to what I call "Red Flags." (See Chapter 9, "Beware the Signs of a Losing Game" for more on this topic.)

At this point, readers have been introduced to the four buying behaviors of companies, the salesperson's position in the buying process (basically in or out), and the style and position of procurement if procurement becomes involved. Note that procurement isn't always directly involved in highly aggressive negotiations. Sometimes these people operate in the background, coaching a senior executive who takes the lead. Aggressive pricing tactics are to be expected from any source. From your understanding of these tactics, you can better prepare your own negotiation tactics and responses. Those tactics are intended to minimize the damage of price-oriented negotiations and to make sure sales isn't wasting company resources pursuing business they have no chance of winning.

The next four chapters present all the details and positioning information you need to negotiate effectively with each of the buyer types. Companies everywhere use sales planning tools, strategic selling, or solution-selling methods, so the goal of Part II of this book is to help you incorporate and fine-tune negotiating actions perfectly targeted to the particular buying type of the procurement adversary sitting across the negotiating table. That's why understanding every wrinkle in the buying center of the customer with whom you are dealing is so critical. This means knowing the incentives, drivers, motivations, fears, budgets, and individuals making up the buying center.

The eight selling scenarios described in the following chapters represent a bulk of the negotiations that most sales professionals will participate in. The scenarios for each buyer type play out differently. One calls for a demonstration of unique and quantifiable value (value buyers). For another, it is all about how close you are willing to shave your margins to close the deal (price buyers).

There is a chapter for each of the four buying types mapped to the two possible scenarios or games that will determine the responses for each buying type, as shown in Table P.1. The two possibilities are that you have a pre-existing relationship with a decision maker at the buyer, or you don't. Whether or not you have such a relationship will, without exception, determine the key elements of your planning, pricing, proposal, negotiations, and follow-up. In general, the scenarios discussed can guide you to begin the preparations much earlier in the sales cycle. The starting point, in fact, begins by mapping out the buying center. Your diligence in sweating these details means the difference between reaping the profits and leaving the profits on the table.

Table P.1 For each of the four buying types, two possibilities—yes, a relationship exists or, no, a relationship does not exist—determines the optimal negotiating behavior.

Customer Type	Existing Relationship	No Relationship
Price Buyer (Chapter 5)	Penny Pincher/Scout	Penny Pincher/Scout
Relationship Buyer (Chapter 6)	In the Pack	Patient Outsider
Value Buyer (Chapter 7)	Player	Crafty Outsider
Poker Player (Chapter 8)	Advantaged Player	Rabbit

Understanding these eight scenarios and the actions you can take to conduct effective price negotiations is paramount to effective selling against the procurement professionals stacked against your profits. Remember, you're in a zero-sum game. The goal of procurement is to grab as much of the pot as possible. Your goal is to hold the line and defend your price against the power of procurement. The following chapters give you the lay of the land. Play your hand well, and you can level the playing field.

Each of the eight scenarios is organized by the following structure: the name, a short description, the tactics that a customer in that scenario will generally employ, and the tactics that a sales professional can use in response, before, during, and after price negotiations.

5

Negotiating with Price Buyers

This chapter focuses on negotiations with price buyers. The one thing that salespeople must truly remember is that price buyers are not looking for value. Price buyers don't respond to offers of extra services. They want only the simplest offer and the best price. Transforming a price buyer into anything else is almost impossible. No matter how many times you go the "extra mile" for price buyers in an attempt to win their loyalty, they will nonetheless organize a multivendor bid the next time they need a product or service. For a price buyer, a supplier is only as good as the lowest bid. Yes, procurement will often handle the purchase here, but there are few games. A salesperson will fill one of two roles. The Penny Pincher will have to be a low cost supplier to be successful here. No high-value or full-featured offering will work for the Price Buyer. There are cases for the purchase of higher risk products and services that even Price Buyers will be loyal to higher value and proven supplier. Salespeople for those firms will fulfill the Scout position—always on the watch for ways to do things better and cheaper.

Table 5.1 The Penny Pincher

Customer Type	Existing Relationship	No Relationship
Price Buyer	Penny Pincher/Scout	Penny Pincher/Scout
Relationship Buyer	In the Pack	Patient Outsider
Value Buyer	Player	Crafty Outsider
Poker Player	Advantaged Player	Rabbit

Price Buyers

All protestations to the contrary, price-buying customers deem price the most important and often, only consideration. They might pay lip service to such variables as value-added features or service enhancements, but in reality all a price buyer cares about is the absolute lowest price possible for a given product or service. They don't care about brands, fancy services, or attempts by the vendor to augment or differentiate the product. All they want is rock-bottom cost. Price buyers will search the world for possible vendors and qualify each and every one. One of the keys to recognizing that you are dealing with a price buyer is that the buyer will have lots of approved vendors—every single one a possible winner if the price is right.

Be particularly cautious in a situation with many vendors. Sometimes multiple vendors could be an indication of a different game than just price buying. For example, a national drug store company might have multiple vendors for pharmaceuticals, but the reason for that is to make sure it gains access to the specialty drugs of each supplier. Sure, it is going to try to leverage the scale and scope of its purchases to get lower prices, but that is not necessarily a pure price buy.

The strategy of price buyers is to establish purchasing criteria and then qualify the largest number of competitive vendors to submit bids. The lowest cost option will inevitably be the one selected. Price buyers are careful not to let themselves get committed to any particular supplier by making sure they are able to change suppliers easily and at will.

An outstanding example of a genuine price buyer is the U.S. General Services Administration (GSA), the agency responsible for purchasing a wide array of goods and services for the federal government. When the Department of Interior, say, needs hand towels for its restrooms, or the Federal Aviation Agency needs desks for its employees, they call the GSA. I have seen many price buyers in my 30-year career, but I have never seen anything like the GSA.

In my early career, I worked as a sales manager for a company in the electrical industry. One day, I accompanied one of our sales representatives as he made a sales call on the GSA. The procurement person couldn't have been nicer. He wanted to show us what we were up against. He took us into a warehouse the size of two football-fields and filled with tables and shelves heaped with goods of every variety. Most of the products I recognized (office supplies, folding chairs, furniture, bathroom supplies, cleaning supplies), but the procurement person had to explain the end use of other products because I had never seen them before. Our guide then walked us over to the electrical section of the warehouse. Again, we saw a myriad of products, including variations of the electrical fittings that my company manufactured. Each of the products had a unique GSA number that identified it as having been verified to meet a set of very exact specifications. We understood that if our products were determined to meet those specifications, they could take their place on the table. All we had to do was submit a bid that was lower than the other guy. Any manufacturer could play this game, and the very nice GSA procurement person was delighted to add our name to the list. The buying decision, he emphasized, would be made exclusively on price. There was no room for taking the procurement person to fancy dinners (federal rules prevent GSA employees from accepting anything of value). We had no hope of developing a relationship. The GSA is a pure price buyer.

Yes, price buyers buy solely on price, but that doesn't mean they are stupid about it. To ensure that their operation will not be disrupted by product shortages caused by the low-price vendor they selected, price buyers usually have high levels of product or service expertise. Most price buyers have internal resources to do the due diligence to determine whether the vendors they select have the experience and reputation to deliver. Price buying is generally handled by the procurement department. If the company requires technical expertise, it tends not to rely on the vendors but rather develops the expertise in-house. Price buyers resist forging relationships with their vendors, and they recoil at paying extra for services. They do not require or want ROI calculations to prove value and differentiation. Instead they rely on specifications set by the production or technical department. With price buyers there's little or no game playing. The focus on price is undisguised.

Some price buyers exhibit a style that suppliers often perceive as very controlling, occasionally to the point of being abusive. Because price buyers resist sales calls and avoid forging relationships with the senior executives of their suppliers, they can seem headstrong and demanding. When I speak at conferences, suppliers sometimes come up to me and say that they sell to a lot of price buyers who don't behave like that. My response is that the most of those customers are not really price buyers, but a variety of value players, a class of buyers that I will explain in Chapter 7, "Negotiating with Value Buyers." Research showed that even in the sale of commodity products, only 30%–35% of buyers were real price buyers. For more sophisticated products and services, the number is much lower—as low as 10% for valued services. That makes sense because there is a risk and cost to price buying—a buyer's cost might actually be higher due to problems with low quality.

The important thing in dealing with price buyers is that you don't kid yourself. Yes, you work for a great company that is intent on doing great things for your customers. Yes, differentiation is a big part of your strategy, and your company has invested heavily in its ability to meet the needs of its customers. Keep in mind, though, that none of this means anything to price buyers. They don't necessarily want and certainly won't pay extra for any of those services you are so intent on providing. So, if you want to sell to price buyers and make a profit, you and your organization had better be a Penny Pincher! If you aren't, forget about it.

Scenario 1: The Penny Pincher

You are selling to a confirmed price buyer. You might or might not have a relationship with the customer. It really doesn't matter. The price buyer regards all the competing suppliers as indistinguishable in terms of their ability to meet the specifications and deliver the product/service. Further, you are often unable to meet with anyone in the firm beyond procurement. In fact, a specific customer policy might be in place to prevent you from meeting with executives beyond the procurement function. Everything in the procurement process is designed to marginalize you as a supplier and often as a person. The suppliers might be kept in a "pen" or waiting room long past appointment times to show you who is in control of this process: procurement.

To succeed in selling to price buyers, your organization has to be a Penny Pincher. This means there can't be any excess cost in your organization. Your operating and personnel costs have to be lean to offer rock-bottom prices. Penny Pinchers tend to source with the lowest possible cost countries and are constantly looking for sources that might be even cheaper. The products or services you sell are true commodities.

Suppliers must be very careful with price buyers. One can easily rationalize granting an extremely low price that represents a loss for the supplier on the basis that it will "make it up in volume." That is, it will make profit in the hope of gradually raising prices and adding additional services over time. This doesn't happen. Instead, the price buyer responds to price increases by switching to another vendor that is waiting in line to adopt the same losing strategy. Some tells to look for which will indicate you are dealing with a Price Buyer are the following:

- Price buyers use a request for proposal that has extensive product and service specifications that include supplier performance requirements.

- Buyers invite many suppliers. The buyer might be willing to identify who the suppliers are, but that tactic varies extensively from one buyer to the next.
- Procurement has absolute control of the process.
- Procurement is unwilling to give you access to other members of the buying center.
- Aggressive negotiations focus on getting to your real bottom-line price.
- Buyers have no interest in hearing value stories about differentiation.
- Buyers have little desire to develop relationships—even with senior executives.

Considerations for How to Price the Deal and the Negotiation for Penny Pinchers

Don't kid yourself. If you really want to deal with a price buyer, you've got to be willing and able to cut your costs to the bone. Some things to think about:

- Conduct an extensive cost analysis that includes all costs of service and support before you develop a price.
- Strip away all value-added features and services in pricing the deal.
- Avoid the temptation to exclude costs that you really won't be able to avoid.
- Consider costing below fixed cost allocations *only* if you a) have excess capacity and b) are able to "bump" this customer when more profitable business comes along.

Planning the Negotiation for Penny Pinchers

In preparation for the negotiation, there are specific facts that will prepare you for being successful in dealing with Price Buyers.

Remember, being successful may mean that you walk away and avoid taking the business at a substantial loss.

Before the Negotiation

- Try to "walk the floor" away from procurement to have casual discussions with other members of the buying center to determine whether they might be poker playing.
- If you can't determine the game, assume you are dealing with price buying behavior.
- Establish a rational walkaway price and get everyone—especially senior executives—to agree with it. Failure to establish a walkaway price increases the likelihood that you will suffer from the "winner's curse." That is, you will win the business at a price that is so low that it will cost you money
- Identify and plan to take away value-added service—don't kid yourself—here they have no value.

During the Negotiation

When you sit down at the negotiating table, two things are likely to happen. First, the procurement point person starts the meeting by telling you that your price is too high. Second, he or she might even share the low price of a specific competitor you will have to beat. You don't necessarily have to accept that this comparison is authentic. The goal of procurement is to play multiple vendors against each other. Even if you win the business, the negotiations aren't over. Procurement will put the "winning" supplier through the grinder in another series of negotiations to drive down price. To counter these tactics, consider these responses:

- Be aware of your total costs (including service) to serve the customer.

- Resist the temptation to get emotionally attached to winning the business at all costs.
- Simplify the offering. Eliminate all value-added features and services.
- Walk away at your identified price.
- If you have justified the low price just to fill excess capacity, make it a short-term contract or reserve the right to "bump" the customer.
- Specify the statement of work in great detail.

After the Negotiation

- Extend the contract only to fill existing capacity.
- Don't expand capacity to service a price buyer unless you are certain that expansion costs are lower than prices being charged.
- Control for scope creep—list the project, time, and resource obligations of each side. "Nibbling" is a common tactic of both price buyers and poker players. Nibbling and allowing project scope to "creep" is a Price Buyer's way of getting more value out of suppliers.
- Charge for extra services requested by the client.
- Refrain from investing to improve the relationship.

Note

If you're unable to use any of these tactics, your firm is going to lose money on this project.

Let me illustrate the futility of "winning" unattractive business by citing a scene from the musical, *The Sound of Music*. Recently booted out of the abbey, Maria is being interviewed by Captain von Trapp for the position of governess for his seven children. Maria is wearing a dress unattractive and dowdy by the elegant standards of 1939 Salzburg, Austria. The Captain wants Maria to meet his children, but her dress is a problem.

> CAPTAIN VON TRAPP: Put on another dress before meeting the children.
>
> MARIA: But I don't have another. When we enter the abbey, our worldly clothes go to the poor.
>
> CAPTAIN: What about the dress you're wearing?
>
> MARIA: The poor didn't want this one.

In other words, be careful about bidding on a business that your competitors walked away from. Do not just assume that your competitors have intelligence to match yours. They might be smarter.

"Once a price buyer, always a price buyer" is a truism that you can take to the bank, but occasionally a price buyer exhibits temporary characteristics of a relationship buyer. Being able to recognize such moments is a good thing because they represent opportunities for profit.

Here's what to look for: a gambit that asks the supplier for some consideration because the price buyer is "in trouble" or "needs a hand." The reason for this behavior is that price buyers sometimes pay the price for their stinginess. They might be out of a critical component, otherwise have difficulties with a product line, or actually be forced to shut down a manufacturing facility because of a manufacturing problem or product shortage. If they were relationship buyers, they would have suppliers who would be willing to go the extra mile for them, but they are price buyers, so they don't have the relationships that come in handy when the chips are down. At this point, price buyers will be desperate and want their suppliers to rescue them.

Price buyers will promise to reward your loyalty by being loyal to you and treating you as a "favored" supplier in future negotiations. The procurement person advancing this seduction might be very convincing. Don't believe any promises about future behavior. If you are inclined to help the "price buyer in trouble," the important thing is to cement the promise in something immediate—a quid pro quo. Price buyers actually respect this display of confidence. You are sending a signal that you are prepared to take care of customers who take care of you. The message will be received loud and clear not only by the customer, but in many cases, by other customers.

What should be the supplier's response to a price buyer who needs a favor and promises future benefits? In a word, skepticism. A price buyer remains a price buyer even when being a relationship buyer is in his company's best interest. Thinking that a price buyer will magically transform into a relationship buyer and treat you as a favored supplier because you offered a good price and "saved" him is a fantasy. Know your leverage and use it in your favor. The more a price buyer needs you, the higher the price you should charge. If you are uncomfortable about "taking advantage" of a customer predicament by increasing your prices, you offer the higher price as an option. For example, you can tell customers that you can certainly help with their company's regrettable predicament and can respond in two weeks for $50,000. When the customer objects that two weeks is too long and that a response is needed within five days, then you counter by saying a response in five days will certainly stress your organization but you can commit to the customer's time frame for $100,000. The choice to absorb the higher price then becomes the customer's.

Many salespeople agonize over dealing with price buyers. My advice is to relax. Price buyers are simply not worth the stress. It's a waste of time and emotion. Real price buyers want vendors that have efficient operations, low costs, and are willing to sell at razor-thin margins, at cost, and if it means a loss for the supplier, even better. If you know your costs and walkaway number, you know whether you can do business. If you can't, just walk away and don't look back. You have profitable customers to pursue. If you are managed and incented to do the right thing for your firm, don't fall prey to the need to close the business unless Penny Pinching is a specific part of your strategy. If it isn't, pointing out the unreasonably low-cost calculations takes confidence. Walking away from the deal takes coolness, and convincing your bosses that this is a reasonable thing to do takes self-assurance.

By the way, another advantage to being willing to walk away is that this tactic is one that is effective against Poker Player buyers. Many of the tactics described in the Penny Pincher scenario will help you be more successful with Price Buyers, but they will also help you distinguish between Price Buyers and Poker Players. If an apparent Price Buyer complains when you take away value, she is probably really a Poker Player. See Chapter 8, "Negotiating with Poker Players," for more information.

Scenario 2: The Scout

Despite what you hear about price buyers, some managers and even procurement people recognize that they need vendors that are able to provide special technologies, skills, products, and services to get their job done. After all, you don't want to have them buying F-22 Raptor jet aircraft from 16 different vendors for the absolute lowest possible price. In these cases, although they are often required by law or corporate policy to buy from the lowest-priced vendor, they are able to legally and ethically manipulate the process so that the right vendor gets chosen for the work. In this case, the job of the seller is generally to be the Scout—the firm that works to make sure that the right things are done for the client. But you've got to do it cost effectively.

You are selling to a confirmed price buyer with the following condition: The buyer is required by policy or law to buy from the lowest-cost vendor. However, the decision makers in the firm have indicated that although they are required to buy based on price, they know that you provide additional value, and they will make sure that your value is given consideration in the final decision process.

Many price buyers are obliged to buy from the lowest builder, as are some businesses. Government procurement at all levels—federal, state, and local—often falls into this condition. Yet despite the policy or law, the individual actually making the buying decision has some leeway, recognizing that some vendors bring a particular strength or skill into the mix. So although the buyer is theoretically agnostic about which vendor prevails, in actuality the procurement process is manipulated to favor a preferred vendor. The process is typically controlled by tightly defining the specifications or limiting the number of bidding vendors.

There is usually nothing corrupt about such manipulation. Many government contractors and commodity suppliers are required to act like strict price buyers. They recognize the need to favor vendors for a variety of rational reasons. A particular vendor might have a new process technology that works better than all others. A vendor might deploy a skill set that is dramatically able to outperform other vendors. Yes, the rigidity of the procurement process officially prevents the buyers from recognizing such differences as valuable, but procurement professionals usually find a legal way to discern and reward value.

If you are a vendor that has those skills or technologies, developing valuable relationships with those particular buyers is possible. Your position has to be similar to a scout in the wilderness. You need to help the decision makers search for value opportunities and prepare a procurement process that meets the letter of the law but permits them to buy the value. Sometimes making some level of profit is done with change orders—this often happens in both construction and military systems procurement. The initial decision is based exclusively on price, but over time, the specifications change, and the supplier makes all changes on a cost-plus basis, which is often where it makes its money.

As the Scout, plan to be continually vigilant for the terms and conditions of the current opportunity, new opportunities, and the need to perform additional activities, often contractual, in order to assure your continued favored position with the buyer.

Assessing the Price Buyer Position and Tactics for Scouts

- The bidding process is positioned not by preference but by law or policy.
- The process is controlled by procurement, *but* the actual decision maker is willing to make the decision based on value or trust in a particular vendor.
- A very formal process of bidding and selection is led by procurement.
- Many vendors might be invited to bid, *but* often a limited number are selected from the bids and put on a preferred vendor list.
- You have an open and honest relationship with decision maker.

Considerations for How to Price the Deal and the Negotiation for Scouts

- The initial solution might need to be the lowest cost.
- You might decide to take the business at a loss or a razor-thin margin.
- Carefully managed projects lead to more profitable cost-plus change orders.
- Incremental value that reduces a customer's operational costs can often be used to justify increased prices.

Planning the Scout Negotiation

If you are in the Scout position, there are tactics to think about before, during, and after the negotiation. The most important thing to remember is that you are still dealing with a firm that will want to initially buy at the lowest possible price.

Tactics Before the Negotiation

- Be very aware of the specific requirements of the bid—dates and details.
- Build the relationship far in advance of the bid.
- Invest in understanding the true needs of the individual and organization.
- Develop a buying center profile and match customer buying center members with members of the selling team.
- Have an in-depth understanding of how your costs compare to all bidding competitors.

During the Negotiation

- Respect and work with the process.
- Lead with your lowest possible price, but also lead with a value discussion for client decision makers.

After the Negotiation

- Collect feedback and new insights during execution of the current project.
- Extend your coverage to additional buying center members and identify new opportunities.
- If the team that does the work is valued by the client, discuss how you can preserve it—use it to leverage into the next bid.
- Always keep your eye on what you need to do to ensure your position in the next bid.

As the Scout, your success is based on your ability to do two things: meet the price requirements and maintain a credible value or relationship narrative with the customer. Consider the following story: Many years ago, I was a regional sales manager for a small company in the electrical industry. Our agent had referred us to a power plant project that included a need for a large quantity of vapor-proof lighting equipment. Our company was not specified; three of the larger vendors in the business were. Our method of production used high-pressure die casting, which allowed us to manufacture the product at a lower cost per unit than our competitors. Our Vice President of Production worked closely with me crafting a low-cost bid—we went through several iterations with the contractor that was building the plant.

Finally, the contractor agreed to let me meet with the project manager at the plant. I flew to the plant with a sample of our fixture. When I walked into the on-site construction trailer and introduced myself, the construction manager could not have been ruder. He grabbed the sample I brought and started disassembling it. When I objected, he told me to shut up. He then signaled me to accompany him as he trudged through the muddy construction site, ruining the dress shoes that I had on. He climbed onto a tall structure that permitted conduit and piping to go over the road trucks used to supply the facility—it was probably only 20 feet high but to me, but it looked like 100 feet—and asked me to climb up with him.

The construction manager pointed to the competing light fixture that was installed in the structure and asked me why the fixture I represented was superior. I took the lid off the competing product and pointed out six specific advantages our product offered. After the most unusual presentation I ever offered, we walked back to the construction trailer. He considered the issue for a few minutes and agreed to place the order with us. Yes, this contractor had to compete on price, and it expected all of its suppliers to do the same, but it was willing to buy based on value. I had to be a Scout to get the job done, ruined dress shoes and all. In this case, I had to be the Patient Outsider, too—something that I talk about more in Chapter 6, "Negotiating with Relationship Buyers."

6

Negotiating with Relationship Buyers

Believe it or not, there are still companies out there that want to have solid, high-trust relationships with their suppliers. Relationship customers rely on their suppliers to take care of them in a particular area of expertise because they elect not to develop that expertise on their own. For example, most businesses believe that hosting their own payroll functions makes little sense when firms such as ADP can offer a more scalable solution better and cheaper. Even though Fortune 500 companies have their own (sometimes huge) legal department, they still rely on an outside, trusted legal firm to handle specialized tasks as due diligence in acquisitions or complex litigation. A large amount of relationship buying even exists for commodity electronics. In these cases, buyers just don't want to be bothered worrying about the quality of their circuit boards and, even though many possible suppliers exist, perhaps even cheaper than their supplier partners, they intentionally stay loyal to one or two suppliers because they value stability and predictability. These customers know they can rely on their circuit board suppliers. When you are selling to Relationship Buyers, you can fulfill one of two positions. If you have an existing and productive relationship, you are In the Pack—you are a member of the team but need to be constantly on the look out for you customer's evolving needs and new, more effective solutions. If you don't have a relationship, you've got to be the Patient Outsider—waiting until the customer's needs change or the current supplier is no longer able to effectively meet them.

Relationship buyers make it simple. It's all black or white, on or off, in or out. With relationship customers you either have a relationship or you don't. You are either on the inside as a trusted supplier or you aren't.

Relationship buyers are probably a salesperson's favorite customer. Salespeople are traditionally focused on caring for customer relationships. Personal friendships often flow out of these customer-supplier relationships. Even so, sales professionals must remember to stay professional. Don't get greedy or lazy in the relationship. You must be continually on the lookout for ways to better support your loyal customers. You never know when another salesperson from a competitor might be introduced into the mix and build a trusted relationship—you will find yourself on the outside looking in. The lesson is to remain vigilant in providing value, creating a satisfied customer, and avoiding giving an opportunity for a competitor to get a foot in the door.

Relationship Buyers

Relationship buyers often look more like partners than mere vendors. Relationship buyers rely on their suppliers to provide the necessary products and services on a timely basis and to be available to answer questions, respond to problems, and help the buyer get out of certain jams. They expect their suppliers to invest in understanding the business their products or services support. To that end, they tend to be unusually transparent in their business practices as well as honest about their difficulties and tend to give suppliers an open look at the purchasing process and more or less unfettered access to the key decision makers. Because such an investment of time and resources is costly, relationship buyers tend to have only one supplier for a particular purchase. The possibility exists that for the purchase of some Original Equipment Manufacturing (OEM) components, a relationship with a second supplier will be maintained as a safety measure, but the bulk of the purchases will go to the trusted supplier.

A key element of relationship buyers is that they often lack expertise in the area that the supplier provides. More specifically, relationship buyers rely on suppliers to provide the expertise needed to make the product or service work for the customer. If that involves customization, the supplier is expected to provide it. I have seen some relationship buyers with moderate levels of in-house applications expertise, but even so they rely on their vendors for advanced support of the specialty area. This scenario is typical in IT outsourcing or financial services engagements in which an internal IT department performs routine service and support function but relies on outside vendors to handle significant projects. As a general rule, the actual decision maker for relationship-oriented customers is a senior executive who usually works outside of the formal procurement function. This executive values the trust-based relationship with the vendor and is willing to invest some time and energy to keep the company-supplier relationship stable. Typically these executives cultivate professional relationships with their counterparts at the supplier or vendor in an effort to avoid problems or disruptions and to be able to resolve them quickly if issues come up.

Further, because the president and CEO positions tend to be more of a generalist role, those executives need to rely on a wide range of financial, legal, technical, and business strategy specialists. Those specialists can be in the firm or an external vendor organization. Wherever those advisors sit, the executive needs to trust them, their insights, and especially their advice. If the advisor is in an outside vendor organization, the executive has a specific strategy to have a trusting relationship with those advisors. Those relationships often last for years and transfer to different organizations as the executive moves around in his or her career. Chapter 7, "Negotiating with Value Buyers," describes how the McKinsey business strategy firm develops and cultivates relationships with senior executives in client firms that start buying based on value but eventually evolve to a relationship buyer when they begin to trust the McKinsey partner.

Several firms in the IT systems business are recognizing that if they treat a customer properly, they can actually change the behavior of a value buyer to a loyal buyer. By focusing on how to make the customer more successful, connecting at all levels of the firm, and giving decision makers data about how they create value, companies such as Hewlett-Packard and Cisco Systems are developing more enduring relationships with their customers. Consumer products giant Whirlpool Corp. has found that if it focuses on making its dealers more efficient and cost effective, it ends up with more productive relationships.

Clearly, with the proper approach and execution, sellers can create dramatic opportunities to generate and leverage loyal customers. Unfortunately, relationship buyers are on the decline relative to economic buyers in this new age of procurement.

The biggest mistake salespeople make is expecting a relationship scenario when the customer has a different agenda. Salespeople sabotage themselves when they assume all of their customers are relationship buyers when, in fact, only a small percentage value such a relationship. More often than not, if the procurement people at your customer's organization see that you want or have a relationship, they will try to use that knowledge against you with poker playing behavior. Chapter 8, "Negotiating with Poker Players," covers this scenario and what to do about it.

Scenario 3: In the Pack

You are dealing with a relationship customer and enjoy an existing relationship with a decision maker who occupies a responsible role with that customer. That decision maker has a high level of trust in and loyalty to you and the supplier you represent. She has confidence that you are responsive, the product is excellent, and that you will be open and honest with her and always take care of her company when the need arises. You have proven yourself over the years and expect to be able to continue to do that in the future. In short, you are viewed as an extension of the client team and always welcome—you are "in the pack."

Staying on the inside requires confidence, competence, and trust between both the buyer and the seller. If you have this, you are like a member of the family. However, it's more than a family. It's a business, and you must work hard to solve its problems and meet its needs. You must be constantly on the prowl for threats and problems, as well as creative opportunities that solve those problems. You know many people at the customer, even beyond the key members of the buying center. When you visit, people are glad to see you and appreciate whatever it is you have to tell and sell them. They know you have their long-term interest at heart because it is also in your interest to do so. They are confident you will not take undue advantage of them for a short-term benefit.

Assessing the Buyer Position and Tactics if You Are in the Pack

The following is a brief description of what you should see from your client if you are truly in that position:

- You have an existing relationship with the decision maker, who tends to have a higher position in the client's firm.

- The buyer is open and honest with you about its true problems, what it is trying to accomplish, and the process it is going through to use your products or have your firm perform work for it.

- The buyer relies on you and your firm to either define or help define solutions with the user and the technical people.

- The buyer tends to have low internal skills in your area of expertise and relies on you to provide those skills.
- The buyer tends to sole source and not use bids in your area.
- However, the buyer might request proposals that list the details and prices of your offering.
- If the buyer uses procurement, it is as a rubber stamp or for finalizing terms and conditions.
- Typically, the buyer is a small or medium-sized business but can be a large firm offering many services or complex solutions such as process control systems.

Considerations for How to Price the Deal and the Negotiation if You Are in the Pack

- Price fairly given the work you do—don't try to leverage the relationship and price high.
- If discounts are available to other customers, make sure they get them, too.
- If you have to discount, only do it once then hold the line on prices.
- Present and quantify a value proposition to defend your position
- Plan trade-offs to give the customer what is best for them.
- You are willing to negotiation contract terms and conditions.
- You are flexible on meeting customer needs and responding to problems.
- You are willing to do things for free—but make sure the buyer is aware that this is what you are doing.

Planning the "in the Pack" Negotiation

In preparing for and executing a negotiation, here are the tactics to consider before, during, and after a negotiation.

Tactics Before the Negotiation

- Develop an intimate knowledge of the client with all members of the buying center.
- Collaborate with the client to understand specific problems, value drivers, and possible solutions.
- Whenever possible, maintain a dedicated account team and/or support.

During the Negotiation

- Focus on making decisions that are in the customer's best interest.
- Any attempt to oversell or do things in your best interest will undermine trust and possibly damage the relationship, so don't do it.
- Whenever possible, provide a complete solution.
- Clients have to know that they are getting the best offering at the best price.

After the Negotiation

- Be open and honest about problems during the work.
- Continually probe for areas of dissatisfaction and the impact of current work.
- Proactively define proposals for new areas of work—identify new decision makers or other problems for existing decision makers.

Selling to a relationship customer is relatively easy. Of course, you have to work hard to really understand not only the stated needs of the customer, but also the unstated or unaware needs, as well. That's what a member of the pack is expected to do. Being a pack member makes discussing buyer needs and finalizing contract terms easier, even though some relatively friendly give-and-take might occur on the terms. Some budget discussions might occur as the customer evolves its business and encounters unexpected ups and downs. Generally, doing business with a relationship buyer is easier than with any other type of buyer.

Scenario 4: The Patient Outsider

You go out and find a customer that wants to have great and trusting relationships with its supplier in your particular area. You want to go rushing in and close the deal, but how are you going to do that? The buyer already has a great relationship with an existing vendor, one with which it is quite satisfied, thank you very much. To be successful in this scenario, you have to accept your role as an outsider and patiently work the customer buying center until the opportunity is right for you to do business—based not on price but on your ability to be a trusted partner to the customer.

The customer is a relationship buyer seeking a trusting relationship with its preferred vendors. The problem is that, for the time being, that preferred vendor is not you. You do not have an existing relationship or a realistic hope of developing one in the short term. One of your competitors is currently encamped in that position, reaping the benefits, and reluctant to give up the privilege.

Recognize that many buyers who value trusting relationships with their vendors have a primary and a secondary vendor for many products. Doing so makes sense for the buyer. The secondary vendor is there to provide a safety net for the buyer in case something happens that prevents the primary vendor from delivering. The secondary vendor usually receives a small portion of the business just to keep it in the buyer's orbit. This is the position of the Patient Outsider.

The Patient Outsider position also occurs when government law or corporate policy dictates buying based on price, yet the decision maker understands the need to buy based on relationship or value from a trusted vendor. If you are on the outside in this scenario, you will also be in the Patient Outsider position.

Is there anything you can do besides quietly waiting for the opportunity to demonstrate your value and perhaps emerge victorious as the preferred vendor? Sure. Go meet with people and introduce yourself and your company. Tell them about what you do and why it is important for them. Sell yourself and your company. Find out about the current vendor and their current needs. Don't push. Ask good questions and be ready with good answers.

My first job out of college was selling lighting equipment. To get specified on a job, I had to meet with and convince consulting electrical engineers who would be designing a building why our gear was better than some of the other suppliers. Sure, I was pretty wet behind the ears and more than just a little naïve. These engineers had great relationships with the seasoned reps from the other suppliers and I didn't get many (okay, any) specifications written. However, I still made the calls, dropped off catalogs, pointed out our new gear, and generally met with people. Sure, they were nice enough, but I still never got any specifications, which is the first step in getting an order.

My boss was a big believer in technical education. When I wasn't on the road, he would hold classes on technical aspects of lighting. He expected us to be to be up on the latest developments in the field. As luck would have it, before I headed out on my week of making sales calls in the north country of New England, I had memorized some technical aspects of lighting. The next day, I was calling on an engineer in Maine, and he made a comment about the efficiency of a particular type of light. The engineer's comment indicated he was not aware of some new developments pertinent to his specific lighting application. Why should he have been aware? I only learned those facts the day before. "Actually," I told the engineer, "recent market statistics show that the efficiency yields are somewhat different." The engineer was more than twice my age. He gave me a condescending smile, as if it were unlikely that the young salesman in his office knew more about lighting efficiency than he did.

He excused himself for a moment, presumably to verify that he was, in fact, correct. To his credit, he came back a bit chastened and admitted that I was, in fact, correct. He rewarded me by giving me a small order for a new building he was specifying lighting for.

Getting the sale took patience, it took doing my homework, and, yes, it even took a little risk to correct him. Not everyone reacts well to being corrected, but by playing the Patient Outsider, I was able to not only get my first specification, but I also formed a productive relationship with the engineer over the following years.

The problem is that waiting for the right opportunity can leave you with the situation out of your control. Sometimes the timing is never right, and you never get a chance. Unless you recognize a customer need that you can uniquely meet, you might have little recourse but to be visible and wait for the current vendor to make a mistake.

Throughout the process, being open and honest is important because that encourages trust. Focus on the aspects of a supplier that build trust: Give of your product and service expertise, show reliability, keep your promises, and ensure that the firm not only meets but exceeds requirements.

Salespeople who find themselves in the role of Patient Outsider need to be careful that they don't get taken advantage of by inadvertently reducing pressure on the primary vendor you want to replace. Yes, you have to show your value, but when that means delivering when the primary vendor cannot, the secondary vendor can ensure that it remains the secondary vendor. The goal is to be the primary vendor. Take care not to pull the other supplier out of trouble without getting your recognition and just rewards from the decision maker. Accordingly, you must have the confidence to refuse to do things such as solving the other supplier's problems all the time. You must have the self-assurance to tell the client that you only provide this special service for your most valued customers. Pricing needs to be handled carefully as well. If you have a high price for a low volume of work and a low price for a high volume of work, a customer will often try to get their safety stock at the low price—promising you more business in the future—which is a version of poker playing. The answer to this tactic is to stick to your guns professionally and charge what you say you were going to charge for the volume actually given.

Assessing the Buyer Position and Tactics for the Patient Outsider

While the customer behavior is the same, since you are on the outside, you will see things a bit differently:

- Relationship buyers tend not to use procurement, but if you're dealing with procurement, it means that you need to get to the real decision maker.

- They will have only one or two suppliers.

- The relationship buyer is open about its real needs and current relationships and receptive to your suggestions.

- If you are able to meet with the decision maker, she will be open as well but might not want to waste her time with you.

- Relationship buyers often have low internal expertise, relying on the current supplier to define services and solutions to meet business needs.

Considerations for How to Price the Deal and the Negotiation

- Be sure to price fairly based on value.

- Never try to buy your way into the account with excessive discounts—it shows desperation at best and at worst, turns the customer into a poker player, and you'll be the Rabbit (see Chapter 8).

- If you do discount, do it once and hold firm in future negotiations.

- Quantify and present a value proposition to support your position.

- Give the customer choices based on different levels of value.

Planning the Patient Outsider Negotiation

If you have no relationship with a relationship buyer when you are involved in the negotiation, you've got to be careful that you still "do your homework" to discover their needs and gain access to the decision maker.

Tactics Before the Negotiation

- Focus on your area of established and known expertise.

- Collaborate with the buyer and the product/service user to discover value needs—especially if you can find unmet needs.

- Wait for some level of dissatisfaction with the current vendor—but it needs to be of concern to users at a high level in the client or the actual decision maker. To some decision makers, a level of dissatisfaction is expected and acceptable.

- Be willing to start small with token work and short-term projects.

- Create relationship matches with different levels of the buying center and members of your firm.

During the Negotiation

If you suddenly find yourself in the middle of a negotiation, you had better ask yourself and the customer why—you might be fulfilling the Rabbit function. However, if you are there because the existing vendor somehow screwed up:

- Focus on your positive aspects and how you can fulfill unmet needs.
- Speak in the client's language—avoid "techno-speak" and feature-oriented discussions—focus on specific value for the client.
- Start the discussion at a level appropriate to the person of highest responsibility in the room—be cautious of lower-level people setting the tone and dialogue when it might be too detailed or not the right focus for the decision maker.
- Price fairly.
- Don't price too low—it will undermine trust, and it is likely that the current vendor will have an opportunity to match. This might cause retaliatory pricing or a price war.
- Make sure you have managed expectations, objectives, and positioning prior to the meeting.

After the Negotiation

- Always stay close to the client—even if it has decided not to go with you.
- Remember, occasionally "checking in" to determine current needs and situations takes patience and willingness.
- Continually and proactively define possible new products and services that might be of value.
- Continually but casually probe for areas of dissatisfaction with the current vendor.

Being the Patient Outsider is difficult and true to its name, requires patience. The pressure to go out and close business is real, but the more you push a relationship buyer, the more you tend to alienate him.

Let me tell you another story about when I was a Patient Outsider. It was at the beginning of my consulting career, and I was anxious to get any work I could to build a client base and keep my small staff occupied. We were always the Outsider to relationships back them, and I lost more business to competitors than I secured. One day I received a call from a large multi-national company asking whether I wanted to bid on a project. After considering it for a few hours, I declined. I was aware that this company had good relationships with several of the large companies that provided similar services, so it seemed to me that our chances were improbable. Furthermore, the customer expected the winning supplier to start in two weeks and provide a complete and implemented solution eight weeks after that. I didn't see how such a schedule was possible; at any rate, I didn't think we could deliver on such an accelerated basis. I said as much to our contact at the customer and concluded by saying we would pass on this opportunity to bid.

Two months later, I got a call from the firm's senior executive in the project. He asked me why I had declined to bid on the project. I told him the truth. I said that I didn't think any consulting firm could be successful under the terms of the project and if he looked at the file, he would see I was quite candid about the matter at the time. As I later came to understand, the consulting firm that was selected, despite its promises, could not deliver on its commitments. Now the company had to revisit the work and needed a partner it could trust. The executive then said the following: "What do we have to do to do business with you?" Well, I got on a plane the next morning to meet with the executive and his senior leadership team. Later that week we started a project at a very agreeable fee and under conditions that made it possible for us to succeed. That project lasted over a year, was very successful, and in many ways cemented our reputation in the industry. The trick to being a Patient Outsider is to be patient.

7

Negotiating with Value Buyers

Simply put, value buyers want value from suppliers—virtually as much as they can get. They have the internal or hired skills to establish performance and buying criteria, evaluate alternate vendors, and make their ultimate decision based on a balanced consideration of both price and value. From the outside, dealing with value buyers might look like just another procurement poker game, but with a little digging, disciplined suppliers can begin to discover who the alternate vendors are and what the process is for selecting them. With value buyers you might work the hardest to win the deal, but you also know right upfront what the stakes are and what you need to do to win. Value buyers want proof of value and how your solutions will make a difference for them. They want to understand the financial implications of your offering. Although they might be loyal to a supplier that has done this work in the past, they won't let vendors rest on their laurels. As with scenarios one through four, with a value buyer, you either have the relationship or you are working to get one. If you are in a evaluation or purchasing process and you have the relationship, you are at the table of the game with a limited number of other vendors that also provide value but usually different levels and types of value. You are a legitimate Player in this game. If you don't have the relationship but are trying to get a seat at the table, you've got to move fast and smart—you're the Crafty Outsider.

Value Buyers

The consideration that motivates value buyers is tangible financial value based on long- and short-term financial return. That is, they favor suppliers who add value to their operations in terms of increased efficiencies, reduced costs, increased sales, and, most emphatically, higher margins. To accomplish these objectives, value buyers are willing to take time to investigate the offerings of alternate vendors to understand the value propositions of each and make calculations about how each vendor is prepared to add value. Value buyers often make their final selection based on their confidence that a supplier truly understands their operation and can add specific value.

For small companies, value buying can be done in a wide range of goods and services where the companies have adequate internal expertise to perform the evaluation of alternate vendors. For larger companies, value buying also occurs in areas such as specialty processing, professional services, and especially IT infrastructure where the supply side is dominated by large and highly reputable suppliers such as Accenture, IBM, and Hewlett-Packard.

Value buyers are often prepared to allow a limited number of vendors to apply their knowledge to the situation. To do that, a value buyer needs to have the internal expertise to determine the validity of what a vendor is proposing. Sometimes that expertise comes in the form of outside consultants and applications experts, even for larger firms, which are much more likely to have some expertise internal to the organization. Of course, to take advantage of the expertise of suppliers, value buyers must have a good understanding of what their needs are to communicate with suppliers.

The individual handling the procurement for a value buyer is often a department manager. The style of these executives tends to be somewhat controlling, but they will generally tell you what their criteria for selection are and advise you on the other vendors and the process for the selection of the winning vendor. In only rare cases will a value buyer have more than three or four vendors approved to supply a particular product or service. The value buyer often focuses on services or the services wrapped around products that can provide value. A value buyer also avoids making commitments that limit their ability to switch to a more valuable supplier. If they do switch, they will want assurances, often in terms of a long-term contract that prevent a supplier from leveraging its position as a favored supplier with higher prices.

Two examples of value buyers are Toyota and Walmart. Yes, these organizations can be brutal in their determination to extract price concessions, but they also have a long history of working with and supporting vendors. As long as a vendor is willing to continuously improve the cost-effectiveness of its partnership with these firms, the vendor can expect its partner to be a buyer that often provides free technical support so the vendors can better do that.

Due to their level of sophistication, value buyers are often the first to evolve their behavior to the next type of buyer, the poker player. Many value buyers learn that if they start playing procurement games, they can get supplies to lower prices for high-value products and services for which they would be prepared to pay more. Few value buyers can resist the temptation to grab money that appears to be lying on the table unguarded. But don't forget value buyers are alive and well and make up a good majority of the buyer mix.

Depending on the industry, dealing with value buyers can be very much like dealing with poker players. If several vendors are determined to have acceptable levels of product and service value, buyers are quite comfortable playing the different vendors against each other to drive prices down. Information technology purchases are a good example of this dynamic. Usually, three to four global vendors sell or have access to leading-edge technology products and have global service and support organizations. Each vendor has the ability to develop and implement sophisticated IT global infrastructure deals. Each suffers from the same need to meet its quarterly numbers, so these vendors are quite adept at discounting to try to close the deal. Inside the relationship or out, these situations are difficult to navigate.

Scenario 5: The Player

You find a customer that wants to buy based on value. You go through a process of understanding its value needs and buying center. You understand that several other potential vendors are in the running. You have some selling to do and will probably have some hard negotiations to do, but you are at least at the table, which is a strong indication that you have a value advantage. You are a Player in the game.

The customer is a value buyer. You have a relationship with a decision maker. The buyer has evaluated different vendors and selected a limited number of suppliers that can meet its needs. Congratulations—you are one of those selected suppliers. It's a very attractive position because you are considered a player in the customer's game. Moreover, you are recognized to have value that, if you are very careful, you can use to leverage that game to your advantage. Because you are at the table with a limited number of competitors, chances are good that you might have the winning hand. Value buyers generally always bring the preferred vendor to the table first—but you haven't won the game yet.

Large organizations are more likely to be value buyers because they have the skills and expertise to identify their problems and define solutions in the long term as well as the short term. Although value buyers might rely on a single preferred vendor to supplement those skills, they know that they can often get more effective and cheaper solutions if they qualify a limited number of high-value vendors to bid for their business. They will often break the business into smaller pieces so each of the valued vendors gets a fair chance to win some of the business. To succeed, be professional and continually look for ways to enhance the relationship *and* the value, and you stand to do well.

As the Player you must keep your game up in regard to demonstrating value—in real dollars. You might have just won the first deal, and perhaps it is a small test to see whether you are a good fit for your customer. The next deal comes along and again, you must demonstrate tangible value with your solution. Please resist the temptation to get overconfident. The game is high stakes. Don't make the mistake of assuming the other players are just as aggressive as you are. They might be more so.

Assessing the Buyer Position and Tactics of the Value Buyer

Note that the Value Buyer position changes little for the Player or the Crafty Outsider, so I have presented it only once.

- Value buyers generally invite only two or three vendors to the table.
- They have specific criteria to evaluate those vendors.
- Value buyers might have a spreadsheet or formula to compare sellers.
- They are open and honest about their needs and occasionally on how they evaluate the competing vendors.
- The value buyers' process will be quite rational and based on sound criteria.
- Their negotiating style might be controlling.
- Value buyers have internal or hired expertise to set criteria and to evaluate vendors.
- The individual that manages and uses will be part of the evaluation and buying process along with other managers.

Considerations for How Price Plays in the Deal and the Negotiation

Again, the rules here are the same for either the Player or the Crafty Outsider:

- Price low, high, or neutral relative to value and those competing for the business.
- After the value solution is locked down, the customer might focus exclusively on price.
- You might have to discount to win the business, but discount carefully and try to connect them to give-gets.
- Present an extensive list of where and how you can provide value relative to other vendors in the negotiation and quantify that value to defend your position.

Planning the Player Negotiation

If you are in the negotiation as a Player with a value buyer, there are a number of important tactics to consider before, during, and after the negotiation:

Tactics Before Negotiation

- Don't focus on price during initial discussions.
- Focus completely on discovering differential value compared to competitors.
- Perform extensive and customer-specific return on investment calculations based on inputs from the buying center.
- Offer choices that take away value for lower prices.

During the Negotiation

- Make differential value your main selling point.
- Avoid non-specific value rhetoric.
- Focus on the application of value to that specific client.
- Continually build trust with open and honest communication.
- If you're forced to discount, employ a give-get strategy.

After the Negotiation

- Even if you fail to win the engagement, continually search for new ways to add value and integrate these insights into your process for future engagements.
- Maintain and provide an expert team to support all elements of the buying center.
- Focus on continually building trust.
- Remain open and honest about problems and possible solutions.

As the Player, your success is based on persuading the customer that you represent more value to the organization than the competition. Success will come from knowing and then being able to persuade the customers, in terms that are immediately meaningful to the customer, that you are superior to every competitor. Value buyers sometimes advance the proposition that all vendors are the same, even if they don't really believe it. They do this because you have failed to differentiate your offering sufficiently. Forcing the conversation back to where you need it to be, value in general, and the particular value your company alone can deliver takes confidence.

Suppose you and your team have just made a terrific presentation and closed it with a complete analysis as to the benefits for the customer. The customer's next question is inevitable: "What's your price?" You smile inwardly because this is a major closing opportunity. However, you don't want to reveal your enthusiasm at this point, nor is it to your advantage to blurt out a dollar sign with a number after it. My advice at this point might seem counterintuitive, but hear me out. You don't want to give the price just yet; rather the next words out of your mouth should be the following: "Are you ready to buy?" Don't let them off the hook on this point because it's absolutely key. *Are you ready to buy?* Your goal is to stick to the value narrative as long as you can. Part of this goal is to defer and limit the price negotiations narrative.

Here's a story that illustrates what I mean about getting the conversation back on track. My company was engaged in finalizing a bid to secure a major engagement with a well-known services business. I knew we were up against a number of much larger consulting companies, but I also knew that our firm offered two points of differentiation that this specific customer valued. I worked hard to force the discussion back to those two points. It wasn't easy, and it required lots of finesse to keep our focus. It helped that we had a sound working relationship with all the executives who had decision-making authority. Because we kept the parties focused on value, we closed the deal without a lot of heated discussion about price. If you have a narrative that works for you, stick to the narrative.

Scenario 6: The Crafty Outsider

Let's say you are selling to a value buyer, but in this case the dance card is full. In other words, the buyer might like what you are offering but has been doing business with two or three suppliers, is satisfied with those relationships, and has little incentive to introduce yet another supplier (which would be you). Navigating this situation, isn't easy, but it's not hopeless. For this scenario, patience doesn't cut it. You could wait forever for one of the favored suppliers to mess up. To get in the game, there is only one thing to do: You must be assertive. You must become the Crafty Outsider.

You are dealing with a value buyer, but unlike the Player scenario, this time you have no relationship with a decision maker. Admittedly, being an outsider with a value buyer puts you in a very tenuous position. Being an outsider has little merit, but a Crafty Outsider is something else. Let me explain the difference. To be successful in the Crafty Outsider position, having extensive knowledge of the various pack of "in" vendors, their skills and weaknesses, and how you are different, helps. My company was recently contacted by a medical devices company to do some standard research—the kind of research done by dozens of market research houses and not the kind of research we do ourselves. The medical devices company had a qualified list of approved vendors. We were clearly outsiders as far as this company was concerned. We would normally just decline this kind of request, but our business development manager noticed an opportunity. He had evidence that the research technique sought by the medical devices company might yield unreliable results in the industry segment it was researching. So instead of just passing on the opportunity, we included a letter with some of the information that made this point. The executive in charge of the project quickly responded. Pretty soon, the executive and our business development manager were exchanging articles and monographs about the research methodology in question.

You can perhaps guess what happened next. The decision maker became intrigued with our firm's take on the matter at hand. It turns out that he was well aware of the shortcomings in the way the project was specified and was impressed not only with our willingness to walk away from the potential work but, without any expectation of reward, to provide real value. In the end, the medical devices company shifted its research methodology and increased its budget to hire us. We were the Crafty Outsider. By being a little assertive (offering a little unsolicited advice), we moved from an outsider to a position as a preferred partner. The trick for us was recognizing that in this customer we were, in fact, dealing with a value buyer.

The bottom line is that we had the confidence to push back on what the customer wanted to do and contend for the business in a crafty manner. It didn't seem to matter that we were on the outside when we started. We still prevailed, and so can you.

The McKinsey consulting company is perhaps the best example of how to play the Crafty Outsider role. McKinsey uses extensive value-based questions to get to the decision maker and eventually settle on evolving its role to the CEO of many of its client firms. McKinsey wants to be in the pack with a relationship buyer. Its total focus is on finding and developing a relationship with the decision maker and building a strong bond as a trusted advisor.

Planning the Crafty Outsider Negotiation

As the Crafty Outsider, you've got to be assertive in the pre-selling process to get your seat at the table. If you are truly able to provide greater value than competitors, don't be afraid to be persistent in your efforts and request to speak with the right people—right up to and possibly beyond when the value buyer has signed the contract with a competing vendor.

Tactics Before the Negotiation

- Probe the customer's situation deeply to understand the real business situation and needs.
- Benchmarking competitive offerings will be critical—make that part of your probing.
- Focus your questioning on areas where you know you provide differential value.
- You will have to work hard for an opening—focus on meeting the users, justifying your value, and working your way to the decision makers.
- Be very cautious that you might be fulfilling the Rabbit position—the easier you get access to procurement, the more likely you will be the Rabbit (see Chapter 8).

During the Negotiation

- You have a terrific benchmark report that highlights your product as better than your competitor. If you are at the table you might be one of two things. You could suddenly be a Player, but be cautious. If you are a true outsider on a value buy, getting to the actual negotiation will be difficult—you might be a Rabbit, too.

- Be focused on value at a reasonable price. Too much focus on price will undermine your position.
- Make sure you have matched different levels of the buying center with individuals from your organization.
- Provide an offering choice package with clearly differentiated value calculations and statements for each.

After the Negotiation

If you win:

- Congratulations—follow the post-negotiations tactics of the Player.
- Maintain and provide an expert team to support all elements of the buying center.
- Focus on continually building trust.
- Be open and honest about problems and possible solutions.

If you lose:

- Continue to interact with buying center members but focus on justifying the need to discuss value with the decision maker.
- Try to develop and present differential value from the winning and existing vendors.
- Be open, honest, and professional throughout.
- Look for small areas where you can begin to prove your value.

Whether you are the Player or Crafty Outsider, good salesmanship is all about getting and defending your seat at the table. It's not as much about negotiating as it is selling skills that focus on getting the meetings, asking the right questions, determining how you provide value, and making sure you sell that value in brief and focused ways.

8

Negotiating with Poker Players

Poker players are value- or relationship-buyers in price buyer disguise. Their intent in acting like a price buyer is to force the negotiation into a bluffing situation that will benefit the buyer at the expense of the seller. Poker players are tricky. They are as much in it for the game as for the discounts they aim to extract. They dress up as price buyers to get the preferred vendor to drop price. They block access to the decision maker. Poker players want endless discounts and hope you will give in. Since the Great Recession these buyers have become even more prevalent. Companies are working hard to cut costs, so why not demand more from vendors? The poker playing is generally handled by procurement. Many procurement managers have developed good tactics to get better prices even though price is not the most important element in the buyer-seller relationship—they just don't tell you that. Their premise to other members of their firm— your real customers is this: "Watch me use my bag of tricks to get them (You!) to drop price." They believe that to win, they have to bluff—and they've learned how to bluff hard.

Let me address readers who are salespeople: If you are hitting the mark, subtracting items and services of value in response to demands for discounts, a poker player will quite likely howl with outrage. A big part of pricing strategy is to hear this howling as welcome music. Let me explain what I mean. With Poker Players, customer objections are a gift. From your perspective, customer objections help strengthen your negotiating position. Through their objections, customers are educating you and giving you something of inestimable value. The more loudly they howl, the more clearly the Poker Players have revealed that what you have proposed subtracting is specifically very valuable to them. Furthermore, the more loudly they object, the more the customers contradict their position that your product or service is a commodity. In fact, it's not a commodity in direct proportion to how particularly they resist your flanking strategy. If you are dealing with a Poker Player, you are in one of two positions. The first is the best one to be in: the Advantaged Player. You have virtually won the business. You have been selected as the best vendor. Now you have to run the gauntlet of procurement. Don't worry: Have some fun, and you'll do just fine. The second position is the worst one to be in. It's a complete waste of your time: You're the Rabbit, there for the entertainment of others with no real chance of winning the business.

Poker Players

Poker player buyers want both value and the benefits that come with having a durable relationship with their suppliers, but they have learned that a certain amount of gamesmanship allows them to get what they want in terms of value but at discount prices. Poker player buyers have learned to obscure their real requirements and bluff with respect to their true intentions in an attempt to manipulate their suppliers into offering price discounts or other concessions. They pretend to be price buyers when they are really not. In other words, poker player buyers have learned that if they focus on price, they can get vendors to offer discounts without compromising high-value features and services.

Some industries actually train their customers to be poker players. Consider the software industry. If you look at the sales charts of a typical software company, the growth curve looks like a hockey stick: nothing for two months and then a sharp increase at the end of a quarter. That's because at the end of each quarter, salespeople and their bosses are desperate to make their sales goals. Price becomes secondary. Customers know this. So what inevitably happens? Sales might get recorded, but margins go to pot. When Oracle was buying PeopleSoft, the industry journals all noted that 80 percent of all discounts that these enterprise software players offered were offered in the last few days before the end of a quarter.

Most buyers want the kind of value that comes with having long-term relationships with their vendors—they know that good salespeople invest in their understanding of how to make their business better. They will work for buyers to get products and projects on time. People generally want to feel good about their relationships in business, but professional procurement people figured out a long time ago that if they adopt the emotionless stance of the price buyer, they might come away with even lower prices. These Poker Players realized that if they understood the motivations and systems of their suppliers, they could probably leverage that understanding into lower prices without sacrificing value. There was a time when the definition of procurement was to simply buy required materials, but that's the case no more. The new definition of procurement is to drive prices down and from that price derive required value. Here the game is guts poker—the ability to bluff to the brink, the ability to push to get the other guy, the supplier, to blink first and discount.

How is a supplier to know when it's dealing with a Poker Player? What, specifically, are the clues that distinguish Poker Players from price buyers? In general, if you encounter the following situations, chances are good that you are in fact dealing with a Poker Player:

- The purchasing process is going smoothly with a non-procurement manager or executive and then you find that procurement has taken over.
- Procurement blocks access to the decision maker and often other members of the buying center.

- The customer has engaged an outside consultant to handle the purchase (the client has outsourced procurement). The premise of the outside consultant is that they can play poker better than you.

- Procurement has adopted a very controlling or kamikaze style.

- New vendors are haphazardly approved.

- The purchase suddenly takes the form of a request for proposal or bid.

- Even the decision maker or manager doing these things is often an indication of poker playing—an attempt to keep the current valued vendor "honest" in its pricing.

What drives the customer to more aggressive poker-playing behavior is the knowledge that lower prices can be had by playing this particular game. This knowledge can come from the Poker Player adding one or more competitors to the negotiation on a haphazard basis. In some segments, industry associations actually post prices paid for important products so that members can make sure they are getting the best prices. Poker Players use this price list as a wedge or a cudgel. Sometimes a new procurement person will be hired who has the general belief that poker playing leads to lower prices.

Poker Players are adaptive. If you develop a new tactic, they're going to figure it out and develop a game that favors them around that tactic. Many sales professionals find staying ahead of the curve to be impossible. To be sure, many sales professionals have failed to adapt while the procurement professionals kept innovating. To the extent salespeople have not learned to play the game effectively, they have actually strengthened the position of their poker-playing procurement antagonists. When salespeople say, "Okay, Mr. Procurement Person, you want a discount? No problem; here it is," they unintentionally strengthen the credibility of the procurement function in the organization and give them even more influence over the buying process.

Just because buyers say they want your product or service at the lowest possible price doesn't automatically make them price buyers.

Of course, the buyer wants to obtain your wares at the lowest price possible price. That's true of every buyer since the world was young. Wanting low prices is just normal buying behavior. Even status-conscious consumers who value luxury goods prefer to pay at the low end of the high prices for their baubles. Poker Players do more than prefer lower prices; they manipulate for it. Price buyers are straight up willing to buy based on price—no games here.

Poker Players employ the tricks of control and deception to keep their suppliers off-balance. They use suppliers' anxiety and fear against them. Poker Players set up the game to encourage the fear and anxiety they can exploit to their own advantage. Your challenge is not to fall prey to those tricks.

In these scenarios your job is to expose their true nature: either relationship buyer or value buyer, and offer them the right package to meet those needs. Your job is also to expose the possibility that you have no shot at winning the business. In that case, you know you're wasting your resources, and it's time to withdraw.

Scenario 7: The Advantaged Player

Has the following ever happened to you? You do the legwork, you identify the prospects, and you find out what customers' individual needs are. You study the business to find out how your company can meet the value or relationship needs of the prospects. You're ready to go in, close the business, and come home with the order. Suddenly someone from procurement shows up and says that he is now responsible for this purchase, and you better sharpen your pencil if you want the business. If so, you know how disempowering it can feel. However, don't get angry and don't fret—get even. Remember, you have power. You are the Advantaged Player.

In this scenario, you are dealing with a value- or relationship-buyer with whom you have a relationship. Suddenly you notice an inexplicable change in behavior. Your normally value- and loyalty-driven customer suddenly starts behaving as a price buyer. You believe that the change in behavior is a procurement-inspired game designed to make you think the customer is now a price buyer in an effort to get you to drop your prices. You are the Advantaged Player.

It's just a matter of time before many value or relationship buyers experiment with poker playing to see whether it yields them an advantage. That's because more and more customer organizations are elevating the procurement function across the enterprise. As procurement professionals get more clout, they are inexorably shifting even traditionally value-buying enterprises into poker playing by exhibiting price-buying behaviors. As they succeed in extracting lower prices and other concessions from their trusted high-value suppliers, the procurement function further enhances its standing, gains more control, and gets better at what it does.

As the Advantaged Player, you must remember two things:

- You already have the advantage. You've done your selling, you've worked the buying center, and you know the decision makers. You're the preferred vendor.

- To win, you're going to have to bluff right back and just as hard. Yes, there is some risk in bluffing back. If you don't have the confidence to bluff back, you are going to lose, and lose big time. Lose what? Profit—as much as the customer can take.

Responding to this scenario is not for the faint of heart. What are the options? You can, of course, simply concede their demands for lower prices or other terms disadvantageous to you. That's what a lot of salespeople and senior executives do because they want to close the deal. That's what the procurement people are hoping for. But doing so validates their tactics and emboldens procurement to make even more demands next time. The other option is to resist, deploying every tactic that this book describes.

Resistance is not easy. Here's where self-assurance comes in. Are you willing to absorb some level of customer dissatisfaction? Are you willing to take the risk of the customer walking? That's what confidence in your pricing strategy requires. That and one other thing: Let go of thinking of yourself as the nice guy. There's no percentage in being nice. What I recommend is an assertive attitude supported by a deep knowledge of the customer's requirements and how your products add value. If you stand on that confidence, chances are that you will do well.

Here's a dirty little secret: Customer satisfaction programs often work against salespeople by undermining their ability to be strong negotiators on their own behalf. Salespeople are sometimes so worried about earning good satisfaction scores that they bend over backwards to accommodate customers. Procurement professionals often use those scores—and the threat of lowering them—against their negotiating partners. I believe that's a perverted application of customer satisfaction. You can satisfy customers by providing a good product at a fair price and supporting it well. Even the best satisfaction scores cannot be sustained if your margins are too low. What you need is a better plan to minimize the havoc price-buying Poker Players bring on well-meaning suppliers who don't know how to play the game.

As the Advantaged Player, keep your eyes and ears open for clues to the true nature of the customer and be prepared with the right price and/or value messages. You've heard a lot of stories from me and other people about negotiating. Many of mine are personal learning experiences that formed the basis for this book. Here's what I've learned: Anytime you're afraid of losing a customer, you are going to lose at the negotiating table, especially if you're an Advantaged Player dealing with a good Poker Player. My main advice in this book is to buck up and get over the fear.

Assessing Buyer Position and Tactics for the Advantaged Player

The view and process for the Advantaged Player is quite different than for the Rabbit. The Advantaged Player has gone through a long relationship and sales process:

- Other sellers are involved, but you have an existing and good relationship with the decision maker and other members of the buying center.

- Additional sellers have been qualified and added fairly recently.

- Often by way of a request for proposal process that is being run by procurement but could be controlled by the decision maker's department.

- Access to the decision maker might suddenly be limited.

- Aggressive/abusive style is designed to throw you off guard.

- While it tends to happen in larger companies, even smaller companies are learning to play poker with valued/trusted vendors.

- Compelling external or internal cost pressures might be driving this move—be careful that the customer hasn't really become a price buyer.

Considerations for How Price Plays in the Deal and the Negotiation for the Advantaged Player

- If you discount, take away value.

- Despite what a customer tells you about everything being a commodity, recognize that you have value and an advantage—don't roll over and start discounting—doing so just validates poker-playing behavior.

- Be very tough on all price and value discussions, even down to terms and conditions.

Planning the Advantaged Player Negotiation

Remember, don't get angry; get even. Keep a cool head through the process. This is a game, and you've got to play it well to get a fair price for the business. Some things to consider during the negotiating process:

Tactics Before the Negotiation

- You need to understand the behavior preferred by the decision maker underneath the poker playing.
- Focus on other members of the buying center to gain insights and information, but remember that the decision maker trumps other, especially junior, players.
- Establish valued give-gets ahead of time.
- Pre-plan tactics that the customers will likely use and an appropriate response to each.
- Try to understand underlying motivations and likely tactics.

During the Negotiation

You've done all your homework. You've worked the buying center and have a good relationship with the decision maker. You know your solution is good for this customer and you've priced it fairly. Suddenly procurement people take over the negotiations and dismiss everyone from the table and start ripping you and your team up one side and down the other. They tell you that they have six other vendors dying for this business and you're going to have to really sharpen your pencil if you want to save this order. Some points to remember:

- If they insult you or your company, get up and leave the meeting.
- If they delay, you delay more.
- Don't be afraid to delay, even if they don't.
- Recognize that discounting just gives procurement more validation and power so limit discounting arbitrarily—always attach discounting to give-gets.
- If you get angry, cool off.

- Call out specifics of their game.
- Don't flinch—practice not having a reaction to what they are proposing.
- Remember: Making no decision is better than making a bad decision.
- Keep the scope and engagement terms brief.

After the Negotiation

- Match effort with the specifics of the contract.
- Be very careful of scope creep and requested throw-ins.
- Poker Players try to take advantage of you using a technique called *nibbling*—always asking for more—often little things. Remember, you need to be professional. Stick to the contract and charge them for the extra things they want. The more they complain, the more you know you are doing the right thing.
- Do not give away products and services—force a change order when additions are needed.

It takes time and leadership for everyone in the selling firm to understand and adopt the Advantaged Player position. The story in the "Redefine Risk" section of Chapter 4, "Getting the Tactics Right the First Time," was a classic Advantaged Player position. The procurement person tried to take over, but we used the right tactics to marginalize her and get her to make bad decisions for the company. She was quietly removed from the discussion. We had a recent situation where the procurement person tried to take over and told our business development person that she had better "sharpen her pencil." My colleague told him that we don't work that way but if he needed to reduce the budget, we would be happy to reduce the scope. What happened? He went away and we got a signed contract.

I have to admit that I've reached the point where I love dealing with Poker Players. I know the games, and I never get desperate. I don't care what's at stake and who is pressing me. I know I have to stay cool, calm, and collected if I want to play at this particular table. You, too, can learn to be as confident.

Scenario 8: The Rabbit

The Rabbit position is the worst position a salesperson can occupy. Simply put, occupying the Rabbit position is almost always a waste of time. If you are dealing with a poker player and do not have a relationship with a decision maker, chances are that you are in the Rabbit position (and there might be more than one Rabbit). Avoid participating in such negotiations—just walk away. Apply the resources to an engagement at which you have a decent shot at prevailing. The Rabbit position breeds nothing but futility.

You either have no relationship with a poker-playing buyer, or you have been trying to develop a relationship with a buyer and they ask you to bid against a preferred vendor. The agenda of the buyer is to get someone else to appear to compete for the business and drive the price down of the Advantaged Player. Because of your desire to do business with the company you fall for their trap, and you become the bait to get the Advantaged Player to discount.

Assessing the Buyer Position and Tactics for Rabbits

Your will see some of the same things as the Advantaged Player but from a very different perspective:

- Procurement appears to run the process tightly.
- Might be managed at a level lower than the decision maker.
- Many sellers are involved—perhaps some mid-tier firms.
- The buyer's apparent focus is on price.
- The buyer has a well-established incumbent seller or two.
- You have no access to the real decision makers.

- Tactics are totally focused on gaming and getting you to bid with a lower price.
- The buyer will work aggressively to convince you to bid.

Considerations for How Price Plays in the Deal and the Negotiation

Negotiation is actually quite simple for the Rabbit:

Don't play the game unless you have good reason to believe you can damage your competitor without eliciting retribution.

Planning the Rabbit Negotiation

The real issue here is that you shouldn't be planning the negotiation at all. You shouldn't be getting excited about the possibility of a new client, and you certainly shouldn't be putting together a fancy presentation. But if you or your managers need further proof, do the following to prepare.

Tactics Before the Negotiation

- Answer the question, "Do we really have a chance of winning?"
- Seriously consider not bidding because doing so is often a waste of time.
- Ask very aggressive qualifying questions.
- Insist on meeting with the decision maker.
- Develop a good understanding of the relationship between the incumbent(s) and the decision maker.
- Establish walkaway terms that include the inability to get information during the bid qualification.
- Focus on making changes on internal policies and directives from senior executives that force you to pursue this madness.
- Count the number of red flags (see Chapter 9, "Beware the Signs of a Losing Game").

During the Negotiation

- If a new procurement manager is assigned to you, you might be thinking you are on equal footing, but you're not. You have no chance of winning this business.
- Stick to a solid negotiations plan—you might as well learn something.
- Reduce the scope if a client is forcing price reductions.
- Stick to walkaway terms.
- Try some aggressive tactics of your own—you might as well have some fun.

After the Negotiation

- Give yourself 24 hours to be depressed that once again, you wasted your time.
- Put a big poster up in your office titled, "Customers I will never submit a bid for" and put this customer on the list.
- Put an, "I told you so," memo together chastising the senior manager who forced you to do this.
- Just don't do it again.

Advanced Gamesmanship

My rule is to never willingly occupy the Rabbit position. Actually, there's one exception to this rule, but it's a risky example of advanced gamesmanship, so I urge caution: Remember, the role of the Rabbit is to provide pseudo-competition designed to get the preferred vendor to drop its prices. If you play your Rabbit position particularly well, the preferred vendor might be forced to drop prices low enough that it gives up all profits, cuts its services, or otherwise degrades its ability in the long term to serve the customer well. That will not only weaken your competitor in the long-term, but in extreme cases might open up a position for you. However, even if that's the outcome and you end up selling to the customer, your position will be continuingly undermined by other firms willing to occupy the Rabbit role against you. It's a no-win situation.

Some years ago, I was a wet-behind-the-ears marketing manager. I got a chance to compete against Westinghouse—at the time it supplied a wide range of materials to Ford Motor Company—on a request for proposal. In my admittedly short tenure with the automobile supply company I worked for, I had noticed that our responses to RFPs issued by the Ford were never accepted. Why, I asked, did we want to invest in such a long-shot proposal? Well, my boss had a policy that we would respond to all RFPs. I didn't know the term *Rabbit position*, but even then I knew there was no chance of my proposal getting anywhere. So in my proposal against Westinghouse, I bid a price that was 20 percent below our cost. I didn't see how Westinghouse could match that price and make a profit.

My biggest fear was that we would win the contract and I would have to explain to my boss that we would have to fulfill the contract at a loss; but in the end, the Westinghouse manager met the price I bid, accepted the business, and took a big loss in the bargain. Maybe it was coincidence or maybe my pricing had something to do with it, but Westinghouse soon experienced quality problems, which gave us an opportunity to pick up some of the work in this area that had formerly gone to Westinghouse. In fact we had a field day cherry picking the most profitable lines that Westinghouse was failing to service effectively. Of course, by the time that business came to us, our price had gone up so that our margins would be protected.

Aside from the unique and rare opportunity to force pain on a competitor, the Rabbit position is a loser position unless you can bid without investing significant time or resources. No amount of justification or rationalization will make it a worthwhile position for you to put real time or energy into the proposal. As for whether or not you are in a Rabbit position, remember that in every poker game there is a sucker. If, as you look around the poker table, you're not sure who the sucker is, it's you. It's the same thing with Rabbits. If you're dealing with a price buyer and a number of vendors and you can't tell who the Rabbit is, chances are that the Rabbit is you.

Understanding your "scenario" is a key element of doing the right thing. The eight scenarios represent the vast majority of the negotiating situations you will likely confront. Study them carefully and you will be prepared for whatever the customer throws at you. Throw it back in the right away, and you will always be in a good negotiating position. I can't promise that you'll be the successful vendor every time, but I can promise you that if you don't understand these negotiating tactics, they will be used against you. You will waste considerable resources responding to situations you have no hope of securing. With an understanding of these eight negotiating scenarios, you can also give yourself advantage and close the business in your favor. Part III, "It's a Negotiation, Not a Surrender," shows you how to do just that.

Part III

It's a Negotiation, Not a Surrender

This part focuses on attempts to rationalize a position because you want to close a deal. The discussion starts with some obvious signs that you are at the table of a losing game.

9

Beware the Signs of a Losing Game

We are all creatures of habit. Over the years, we've all picked up some bad habits. One of them that hurts us in selling is denial. Denial in that we fail to see the warning signs associated with a potential pieces of business: We just flat out ignore them. Along the way, we kid ourselves about the chances of winning a piece of business. The trick is to recognize a warning sign or red flag for what it is—an indication that you've got a problem with what you're doing and you need to rethink what you are doing. Negotiating with backbone is about doing things better and smarter. We've spent the past four chapters looking at the tactics of better negotiating. This chapter is about making sure you aren't still in denial about which scenario you're in and the subsequent tactics you're using.

Shortly after Alan Mulally joined Ford Motor Company in 2006, he convened his first staff meeting. He asked every department leader to prepare color-coded charts that would show him to what degree they were tracking goals. At the meeting, he saw 320 graphs. All 320 graphs were completely green, indicating that every project of the part of the company was on target. No exceptions.

Mulally, who left Boeing to take on the CEO position at the troubled automobile company, looked incredulous. "The finance department tells me that we will lose $17 billion this year," Mulally announced. "Guys, is there anything that's not going well?" With that, Mulally sent an unmistakable signal that this was a CEO who wanted to hear the realities of the business: the good, the bad, and the ugly.

At the next staff meeting, those 320 reports weren't all green. A goodly number of them revealed a significant amount of yellow and even the occasional splash of red. With everyone prepared to face hard truths, Ford could actually begin to rebuild for the future. Mulally's practice of having painful, reality-based conversations paid off. Ford announced profits of $2.4 billion in the second quarter of 2011, and the company has paid down $23 billion of debt.

Don't Kid Yourself

Business success demands the exposure of hard truths, but not every business has the culture to accept such exposure. We worked with a large company that sells specialty packaging solutions to assist with the firm's emerging pricing strategy. The company is successful and works hard to bring innovation to its products and services to support the needs of its diverse clients. A senior executive I'll call Elizabeth asked for my help in defending her company during an upcoming negotiation with its largest and most-valued customer. Her instructions to me were two-fold: Preserve the account and protect its already razor-thin margins. Failure, as they say at NASA, was not an option.

Elizabeth was particularly concerned because her customer had recently been acquired by a much larger firm that was known to be a traditional price buyer. She was rightly concerned that while the company she had been dealing with was a relationship buyer, it was likely that the acquiring firm's buying philosophy would become the new normal. To make matters worse, packaging procurement had been relocated from her customer's location to central purchasing at the parent organization. Thus many of the relationships Elizabeth had so carefully cultivated over the years were no longer available to her. To complicate matters further, her firm had never done business with the parent company, no doubt because she was regarded as a high-priced vendor.

The parent company requested all of its packaging vendors to prepare full-blown proposals. Doing so would require considerable resources followed by rounds of negotiations with the top-scoring vendors. Elizabeth was panicking. "Reed, I fear we're going to lose our largest customer," she told me. "What can we do to maintain the relationship without cutting our prices so low that even if we keep the business, we'll lose money servicing the customer?" She was clearly anticipating a brutal negotiation and looked to me for any negotiating tips I could offer that would level the playing field even a little.

My response was short and, no doubt, it felt brutal. "Elizabeth, I'm sorry to be the bearer of bad news. Under the circumstances, I believe it would be a waste of time and resources for you to try to hold on this business," I replied. She looked pained to receive this advice. "I'm sorry," I continued. "I know it's a huge blow to lose such a large customer, but all the cards are stacked against you." I laid it out for her. Her relationships with the old company were no longer of value. The new decision maker did not have an advantageous relationship with Elizabeth's firm. In fact, to the extent it considered Elizabeth's firm at all, the new company considered it a high-price supplier. In the unlikely event Elizabeth's firm competed for the business and was actually retained, it would have to do so at prices it couldn't service at a profit. "Unless your customer changes its buying strategy in the next few weeks, I'm sorry to say that your best strategy is to abandon this account and use the considerable resources you would have spent trying to protect it to obtain replacement business," I concluded.

At moments like this—when consultants advocate painful and unpopular courses of action—is when consulting firms earn their fees. Yes, I know all the jokes about consultants: that consultants just tell the client whatever the client wants to hear, and that consultants borrow the clients' watches to tell them what time it is and then keep the watch! Occasionally, though, consultants actually look at a situation with unvarnished eyes and call it as they see it. I knew the medicine I was prescribing would not go down easily.

My recommendation troubled Elizabeth. Heck, I can't remember a client getting as mad at me as Elizabeth did. In fact, she was so angry with me, she terminated the relationship. I was ready for this eventuality and didn't take it personally. I knew she was under a tremendous amount of pressure to preserve the account. I saw clearly how the endowment effect (explained in Chapter 3, "Stacking the Deck in Your Favor") was operating here.

From some well-placed contacts elsewhere in the company I kept track of what happened next. Elizabeth redoubled her efforts to keep the customer. She assigned a team of her highest-paid staffers to prepare a big presentation documenting why the company should keep its specialty packaging business with Elizabeth's company. In the end, all that effort was to no avail. She couldn't even get an audience with the decision maker to present her argument. Price buyers don't care about evidence, and they certainly don't want to argue.

Yes, Elizabeth did have a chance to participate in the next bid cycle. For price buyers, the more bidders, the merrier. She cut her prices to bone, but given the company's price structure, she wasn't able to drop prices enough to win the business. The customer awarded the business to its preferred vendor for low-cost packaging.

Do I like to lay out the reasons why sellers should probably give up calling on a customer and move on to greener pastures? No, of course not. No one likes to offer bad news. I recognize that salespeople are eternal optimists and resist discouragement. They think if they can just be kept alive, there's hope they can somehow win the business. However, we live in a world of limited resources. Red flags are those little indicators that in spite of all the optimism and denial, you're probably wasting your time. Red flags are indicators that you need a dose of reality. A big one. I explain that cutting your losses and reassigning the marketing resources to securing business that you can serve at a profit is simply prudent. Otherwise, taking that business at a loss is the same as shipping a pack of $20 bills with each order.

Many times salespeople are pushed to pursue bad business by senior executives who need their own dose of reality. Heck, give them one if they need it. If they don't want that dose of reality, you've got a bigger problem on your hands.

Get a Devil's Advocate

I recount the story of Elizabeth to underscore how difficult it is to accept the hard truths that you are playing a losing hand in a sales negotiation that you will not win. Playing the hand out is easier in some ways than folding and moving on to another table. Yet doing so in the face of red flags squanders time and energy that can be more profitably applied to negotiations that you actually have a chance of winning. That's why I suggest every substantial sales negotiation team should have someone acting as a devil's advocate. A devil's advocate is someone who, given a certain argument, takes a position he or she does not necessarily agree with just for the sake of argument. In taking such position, the individual taking on the devil's advocate role seeks to engage others in an argumentative discussion process to illuminate the situation. The purpose of such process is typically to test the quality of the original argument and identify weaknesses in its structure. Typically, the stance is seen as unpopular or unconventional, and that is precisely why a devil's advocate is needed.

Note

The Catholic church originated the concept of the devil's advocate to argue against the canonization of candidates for sainthood. The job of the devil's advocates was to take a skeptical view of the candidate's character, look for holes in the evidence, and argue that any miracles attributed to the candidate were fraudulent.

Before they invest huge sums in a sales negotiation, businesses need someone to play the role of devil's advocate. For obvious reasons, many companies use consulting firms for this purpose. Having an outside perspective that only consultants can offer often helps. Other organizations assign a staff member to play the role of questioning whether the investment in a particular sales negotiation is justifiable given the red flags.

Beware Red Flags

As I said, *red flags* are circumstances that indicate trouble with the account and predict that the vendor's time and effort in putting together a proposal will not be rewarded with a contract. When two or more red flags exist, I tell salespeople they shouldn't bother making an investment in pursuing a possibility that is almost surely elusive. The more red flags that are evident, the more likely it is that sellers are merely occupying the Rabbit position. (See Chapter 8, "Negotiating with Poker Players.") That is, they have been added to the evaluation process not because they have a chance of securing any business, but solely for the purpose of increasing competition and thereby bringing down the price of the successful and usually incumbent vendor. Of course, if the cost of preparing a proposal is minimal—as in the case of dealing with a true price buyer who really wants nothing more than the price bid—a vendor has little to lose. In other situations, you must carefully watch for those red flags.

The following sections describe some of the more common red flags that indicate the salesperson is in a poor position to secure the business.

Customers Have No Experience with You or Your Firm

If the customer has no experience with a vendor and that vendor is added to the bid list anyway, then there are only two reasonable conclusions: Either the customer is on a fishing expedition to see how the vendor responds (a fishing expedition is when procurement throws a baited hook in the water just to see how vendors respond; it is a curious test rather than a serious attempt to buy something) or the customer has added the firm to the bid list as a Rabbit in an attempt to shake a few shekels from the preferred vendor. In any case, responding with a proposal is not in your company's best interests. Review your own RFP history. Are you winning even 5 percent? In these cases, use the newness to your advantage—ask the customer why you have been added and then qualify, qualify, qualify. (See Chapter 4, "Getting the Tactics Right the First Time.")

Procurement Runs the Process Tightly

Procurement controls the buying process because it doesn't want the vendor to snoop around and find the real decision maker. This tactic indicates you're dealing with either a price buyer or a poker player. If the customer is a price buyer, you must first determine whether you can make any money at the account. Don't kid yourself here. Don't think you'll make it up in volume or over time. Some famous last words in sales are that "history is littered with unprofitable deals." If the customer is a poker player, this is an indicator that you're in a game, and you will either walk away or play very carefully. Any time procurement people run the process tightly, they are keeping you from the real decision maker, and I guarantee you that some type of decision about a preferred vendor has been made. The one exception to this might be when negotiating for regularly purchased products—where procurement has a tight series of specifications—but even in these cases, they are just shopping for a lower price.

The Process Is Controlled at the Manager Level

Fishing expeditions done by buyers are generally assigned to lower-level people who might even be open and honest with you and give you great information. These low-level managers might say they and the rest of their team love you to bits, but a strong chance exists that they will be overruled in terms of both process and decision, and you will have wasted your time. Even if they say they will be making the ultimate decision, you must find out who they report to and what relationships that senior executive might have with your competitors. Yes, this is a borderline call. I've seen managerial-level people able to make decisions and control fairly large budgets, but those cases are not only in the minority but also extremely rare. We've been hood-winked by well-meaning managers more times than I can count.

If you are dealing with managers, keep in mind that they don't have much authority in the firm. They don't control a big budget, and they answer to people who do have the authority and control the big budgets. In many cases, those senior people have relationships with vendors that they want to see considered in the process and in most cases selected to do the work. If you aren't that preferred vendor, despite what the manager says, you probably won't win the business.

Buyer Has a Well-Established Incumbent

If, after you are asked to provide a bid or quote, your request to meet with the decision maker is rebuffed, a high likelihood exists that the buyer has a well-established incumbent vendor. Having such an incumbent in the picture is a huge red flag because this vendor has the inside track, and even considerable effort might not dislodge it. Such effort might get the incumbent to lower its prices, but that does you no good, at least not in the short term. Making a competitor lower its prices to such an extent that its future viability is threatened might have long-term benefits, though.

Tim told me that his company would be participating in the reverse auction against not just one but two preferred and well-established incumbents. To me, this was a big red flag, and I told him so. Tim privately agreed with my prediction that his company didn't have a chance of winning the business, but he told me that he couldn't convince the executive team that the best course was to pass on this opportunity. So the company invested the time of a small team for a week to supervise the bidding process. They watched the price get lower and lower. Every time they bid, one of the incumbents matched it. Finally, Tim's company got to a point that it couldn't take the chance of "winning" the auction. Had the company prevailed, it would have lost money on every transaction. The result would have been the very definition of a Pyrrhic victory: Another such victory and we are done for.

Sales Is Unable to Get to the Decision Maker

If a salesperson can't get a meeting with the decision maker, assume that a well-established incumbent exists and ask more qualifying questions. With mature buyers, that's usually the case. The prior story of Tim makes this point, too. Remember, he was a Rabbit in a reverse auction. (See Chapter 4, "Getting the Tactics Right the First Time.") Unlike in an ordinary auction, in which prices increase over time as buyers compete to obtain a good or service, in a reverse auction sellers compete to obtain business, and prices typically decrease over time.

If sales can't even get the decision maker on the phone, much less obtain an in-person appointment, the account is DOA. This is a major and usually insuperable red flag. It doesn't matter what the buyer says or promises. Pursuing the business under these conditions is the most predominant mistake made by vendors in the Rabbit position. When I meet with clients who complain about their low close rates on proposals, my first question is, "How many times have you met with the decision maker in the past three months?" Usually, the answer is zero. Sales tried and tried but never did get such a meeting.

My next question usually answers itself: "Are you able to have a meaningful discussion with the decision maker?" Under such conditions, responding to RFPs is essentially a waste of time. The only response is for sales to be more discriminating, to respond to fewer proposals, and then to respond to only those it has a chance of winning by virtue of there being no red flags.

If you are uncomfortable at the thought of employing some of these tactics, just think about the game and how you need to best play it. When you are at the negotiating table, don't play into the buyer's hands and use panic pricing. Just be a cool, confident professional. If you are unsure what to do, it is better to do nothing than pull the panic pricing lever.

My counsel to sales professionals that they should decline to submit proposals to engagements that have too many red flags is not universally accepted. By nature, salespeople are optimists. Any time they are invited to participate in a bid list, they tend to celebrate. Some sales managers make it policy that sales people must respond to every RFP from a client or prospect. "You're gonna miss every swing not taken," is the mantra of these sales managers. My response is simply to demonstrate with convincing evidence that organizations that follow a "no Rabbit" strategy have better outcomes. Their costs go down, they don't waste time pursuing bids that they have no chance of winning, and they can concentrate their resources on those engagements that they actually can close at a profit. When organizations actually implement such a policy, customer satisfaction increases because the company can free up customer service resources that were otherwise committed to the wasteful pursuit of fruitless business.

Buyer's Focus Is Only on Price and Says That All Products Are Commodities

Salespeople who are extremely good at showing value and developing relationships too often misread the sudden shift to when a buyer's focus is only on price or insists that all products are commodities. This is especially true for high-value products and services. A procurement professional takes over the buying and drives prices down—at least the initial gambit is almost always a bluff. Procurement wants the high-value products and services at a lower price. This is a red flag that a) you have already been selected and b) you are in a poker game but still have the winning hand. Their initial gambit to the Advantaged Player is that all products are commodities, and the main focus is on price. Usually, suppliers fall prey to the tactic. Many of these high-value businesses, suppliers have given up and provide their products wrapped with lots of services at extremely low prices. If so, they have already lost the game. Had they observed the red flag at the start of the storm, they might have offered a stripped-down product to be the low-cost provider to avoid the damage of excessive price competition.

So what's the most effective response to a procurement professional who trots out the objection that the product the salesperson is selling is a commodity?

First, salespeople must recognize the red flag that it is, in this case, a probe in the procurement game. The procurement people are looking to see what the salesperson does next. Second, the best response is for the salesperson to document impeccable understanding of the buyer's business, opportunities, challenges, and how, specifically, it uses the product or service in question as well as what the buyer likes about it. If the salesperson does not have that understanding, it is imperative, to the extent possible, for the salesperson to disengage from procurement and spend quality time with the end users. In most cases, such an investigation will reveal two things:

- That the product or service isn't really a commodity after all. The company derives measurable value from using the product or service in a way it could not obtain from competitive products and services at the equivalent price.
- That the supplier provides measurable added value in terms of technical support, maintenance, customer service, or other services.

With that kind of measureable evidence of value salespeople can convincingly advocate for the prices they believe their products and services merit. With evidence, the game is no longer about bluffing. It's about understanding and leveraging your position.

Red flags pointing to you being in the Rabbit position indicate that you're just wasting your time and the resources of your firm. You are better off doing something productive. On the good side, this last red flag indicates that you are in a better position than you think. Here you've got to use the tactics of the Advantaged Player and protect your value and profits.

10

The Realities of the Game

The prior chapters gave you some good advice and hopefully instructive stories. I know that advice works because I've been using it and giving it for twenty years. I've studied the field of procurement, talked to procurement people, and taken some of the same classes they've taken to learn the tricks that we've talked about. In the game of procurement, there are some realities that we've all got to deal with, and I want to leave you with a few bottom-line pieces of advice.

Sometimes You Have to Discount

Yes, there are times when you just have to discount. It does happens to the best sales professionals. I did it when I was a salesperson, and on occasion I still have no choice but to discount. In my present position, I'm more fortunate than other salespeople because my clients know I'm a pricing expert, and they have some expectation that we of all companies know how to avoid the damage of price negotiations. Believe it or not, just that recognition gives us a measure of control to resist discounting. When we are dealing with senior executives at clients, they comment that they know getting a discount from us will be tough—so they often don't try. But the realities of selling are that sometimes you just have to discount. When I do, I try to understand the root causes of the need to discount and react appropriately. If the customer has a real budget limitation and you have to discount to get the work done properly and you've got some excess capacity, then discounting is appropriate. But you've got to make sure you'll make a profit, even if it is a smaller one than usual. Do what you can to adjust scope or offering structure.

But if you've got to discount, just try to do it less. We've learned from the stories in the book that there are ways to reduce the likelihood of having to discount and the need to go to a middle ground rather than going to the maximum discount. If you can just discount less, it will have a dramatic positive impact on the profits of your sales for your company.

More often, procurement people try to get us to discount and fail. It's how companies do business these days, even in high-value professional services. But because we've focused on assessing the tactics that procurement uses against us and possible solutions, we've learned how to blunt those tactics. We had one situation where we had gone through an extensive project opportunity assessment with a software company. Our business development person got agreement on the project from the people on the client committee and from the decision maker. Procurement people then stepped in, saying that now was the time to put us through the negotiations wringer. The game had changed to poker, but we were the Advantaged Player (refer to Chapter 8, "Negotiating with Poker Players"). They called our president, Carolyn, who had had time to think about what to say. When the procurement person called for a price reduction, she said no problem and advised him that she could cut $25,000 out of the project by changing the client value discovery interviews from person-to-person to telephone. She also told him that he was going to have to send us a note indicating that this could impact the quality of the results and that he would take responsibility for that. She also told him that we thought that due to the number of segments involved, his company wasn't doing enough interviews. The bottom line was that he agreed to the extra person-to-person interviews to improve the quality at an added project cost of $50,000.

Remember: It's called a negotiation, not surrender. Carolyn didn't surrender and didn't get nervous. Here's a little secret for you—we did need the business. We had the capacity, and she wanted to get that order closed, but she didn't panic and pull the discount trigger. She acted like the Advantaged Player she was. She provided a give-get, the justification for it, and sold additional interviews that had considerable value for the client. She didn't surrender. So should and will you if you just remember some of the ideas provided in this book.

David is the vice president of procurement at one of our clients. He is a smart and capable guy who heads the association of procurement professionals in his country. We were putting together some training for his sales professionals, and I wanted to get his ideas for some tactics to use with procurement people. He had already prepared a three-page report on the things they were doing wrong and what they had to do to improve things—and we were very much on the same page on what had to be done. One of his main points is that when he is involved with a purchase contract for his firm, he often asks for a 10 percent discount but expects 5 percent. He is absolutely amazed at how often the salesperson or, in his case, an executive, quickly agrees to the full 10 percent.

Here's what I want you to do. Write the following on a sticky note: Don't surrender—negotiate. Post the note on your desk lamp or wherever you will be sure to notice it. If you are on the road, take another one and attach it to the dashboard of your car. Constantly remind yourself that if you must discount, do it reluctantly and only a little bit at a time. Always try to connect the discount to value. If you are forced to discount, do it thoughtfully and slowly. Always understand the point of the middle ground and try to shoot just a little bit before it. If the client wants 10 percent, make a couple of fake phone calls, run your computer a bit, and agree to give 3 percent. When the client comes back asking for 5 percent, give 3.25 percent. Wear clients down like they are trying to wear you down. Every 1 percent more you can get out of an order goes right to the bottom line for your company. If your firm has a 5 percent net profit, that 1 percent means a 20 percent increase in profits. That's why having backbone in negotiating is so important; it has incredible leverage in improving the profits of your company.

Remember a Simple Checklist

Good account tactics require an understanding of the situation so you can invest your resources wisely. Sure, just responding just the way the customer wants you to is easy. The eight scenarios and following tactics take some getting used to. So here is a simple checklist that will help you figure out which scenario you are in. In the end, your ability to determine the scenario impacts the time and energy of yourself and others and can be a big expense to your firm. Keep the following checklist in mind when you are getting ready for a negotiation:

- Understand your position.
- If you don't know your position, do your homework—ask qualifying questions from a wide range of people in the customer's buying center to find out what their behavior and your position really are.
- If you have a policy that requires you to do the wrong thing, work on getting the policy changed.
- If a senior executive is forcing you to do the wrong thing, get working on your resume. His company is going to lose at the game anyway.
- If you don't have the time to do the right thing, then you will waste your time doing the wrong thing.
- Don't take the process too seriously; after all, it is just a game.

A word about the last rule—yes, I know that your job is at stake, and there are all sorts of people around you who are excited about the business opportunity. I know you have a quota to meet and you are being pushed to pursue a bad position. However, when you get emotionally involved in a position, chances are you are going to do the wrong thing. Procurement wants you to participate when you shouldn't. They want you to discount. They want you to get angry and do the wrong thing for your company. If you can remember that the negotiation is just a game, you'll do just fine.

Develop Your Playbook

The scenarios presented in this book are useful ways to interpret your customer's situation and develop the most appropriate sales negotiation strategy and tactics. Those tactics are designed to minimize the damage of both wasted time and excessive discounts. My intent is to give you enough insight and detail so that you can drive more effective customer approaches. Successful organizations are learning organizations. Some people assume that the recession will pass and things will return to normal, and the pressure from procurement will go away. That they'll be able to develop those nice cozy, high-price relationships with customers that value the services and products we so willingly provide. Here's the wakeup call: The pressure from procurement is not only the "new normal"—it will get worse in the future. Procurement organizations will continue to get better at wringing price concessions out of sellers irrespective of the state of the economy.

Procurement people will get better at what they do. They will get more sophisticated in the techniques they employ. They will get better at reacting to the tactics that salespeople employ. They will gain control in their organization and move beyond rubber stamping to developing sophisticated processes that all salespeople will have to go through to do business with the company. The new normal will actually be worse than it is today—more aggressive poker playing and use of Rabbits to achieve desperation pricing from preferred sellers.

This book is the start of scenario-based selling. In addition to identifying eight primary scenarios, it has focused on two of them that are most damaging in selling situations. However, to keep up with the continuing evolution and development of the procurement function in your customer organizations, salespeople, sales managers, and senior executives must make a concerted effort to develop a continuously evolving playbook of approaches, responses, and tactics to use against procurement.

Developing such a playbook will be a life-long process in successful organizations and the focus of meetings and discussions. This process should evolve and get better over time, and focus on keeping up and getting ahead of the evolution of procurement techniques. You should learn from the mistakes, celebrate the successes, and put them into the playbook so that everyone in the firm can use the information to minimize the damage of customer negotiation.

Don't Be a Victim

One of the most important lessons my father gave me was, "Don't be a victim." He did not believe in being victimized by circumstances. If I was afraid of something, I had to figure it out and deal with it head on. For example, I am afraid of heights. Put me on the rooftop of a tall building and the superman cape doesn't come out, the panic does. Several years ago I had a tree to cut down in the front yard. My parents gave me tree-climbing equipment for Christmas. It was a not-too-subtle signal to confront my fear by felling the tree. Late one afternoon, I put the climbing spikes on my feet and climbed the tree. I only climbed about three feet of it before the fear got to me and I backed down. The next afternoon I probably got up to six feet. After about a week, I was high enough that I could get the job done. Since then I've climbed and topped a lot of trees. Am I still afraid of heights? Yes—but I have learned how to manage my fear, and I can generally get the job done if I need to.

What's the point of this story? Salespeople are often victimized by the tricks that procurement plays on us because we are afraid of losing the business. They do something that appears to threaten the order, and we cave, granting the discount. I see it with salespeople and executives all the time. They are victims of circumstances. They are caught between the rock of sales goals and the hard place of procurement, and they don't have a way out. They rationalize those circumstances by saying that discounting is part of their industry practices or that they chose to "invest" in the relationship. They don't think it's possible to do it any other way. They wring their hands when they talk about the pressure to discount. They are totally victimized by the circumstances of their businesses and the games their clients play.

Being a victim says that you have to react to the request—that you have no control over the process. It is an attitude of defeat. It causes you to believe that procurement has already won the game and there is nothing you can do but discount your firm's profits away. In negotiating, being a victim is the worse thing you can do. It lets procurement dictate the terms of how you do business.

Get Some Backbone

There is a better way to negotiate than being a victim. The first step is to recognize that you are being victimized. Don't rationalize, recognize. Don't sugar-coat the circumstances; figure them out. The second step is to understand that this process is not about letting business go. It's about being willing to let business go. The difference is subtle, but important. That willingness to let business go gives you the professional confidence to be a better negotiator and get the price you deserve in a way that makes you feel better about who you are and what you do. That confidence comes from recognizing that if you walk away from an opportunity or a bid, you had zero chance of winning it anyway and you were just wasting your time. Or if you walk away from a negotiation because you've hit your walkaway price, it's because you have a lot of power and you are just exercising it. Your confidence is based on recognizing that the purchasing person is sweating the negotiation just as much as and maybe more than you. Having confidence is about not being a victim. It's about climbing that tree.

It's also about taking some control of your professional life and doing the things that need to be done in the best interest of your organization. The thing that we all fear is losing a piece of important business. Procurement people use that fear against salespeople. That is not an exaggeration—it is a concrete fact. To become a better negotiator, you must get over that fear—not because you are going to lose the business, but so that the fear you will lose the business doesn't cause you to do things that undermine both your profits and your sense of worth in a business.

The purpose of the scenarios presented in this book is to give you eight situations to consider when you are in or trying to develop a relationship with a customer. They are described so that you have some sense of your specific situation and the game you must play. If you can't seem to figure out your situation, roll your shoulders, take a deep breath, and try to figure it out. Talk to other people to sort through all the signals—heck, send me an e-mail and I'll help you. You do have to figure it out. If you can't, you're screwed anyway. However, if you can slow down, think about your circumstances, and figure them out, you've completed the first step to becoming a better negotiator.

Lack of understanding of your situation and fear over losing a piece of business leads to panic pricing. Panic pricing is pulling the price discount lever too often, too much, and without thinking about the alternative. It's what my mom did with the car salesman—when at 86 years old, buying her first car, she used two of the tactics I talked about in Chapter 1, "Tough Selling—the New Normal." The car salesman (and his vice president of sales) both pulled the panic pricing lever. They were afraid of losing a customer and pulled the lever because it was what they did, especially at the end of the month when they were desperate for business.

Take a pledge not to pull the lever. Before you even get to that point ask yourself a question: "Am I afraid of losing the business?" If the answer is, "Yes," then stop and think about your situation. If you don't know your situation, chances are you have no relationship and you are being played as a Rabbit, so just walk away. Don't waste your time and promise to do better next time. Spend time analyzing which scenario you're in and look at the appropriate tactics. Talk about your selling situation with other salespeople and your managers. Just don't pull that panic pricing lever until you've had a chance to make sure it's the right thing to do.

What do you do if you have a manager or executive pushing you to discount? I find that being rational is a good start. Try to point out the problem to the executive and get him and/or the situation to change. I know that sometimes this is just impossible. Believe it or not, we struggle with this one ourselves. Employing the tactics discussed in this book has taken years for us as a team to learn. Don't kid yourselves—getting everyone working on the same page is going to take time, patience, and leadership.

I work with a lot of professional salespeople, though they often have fancier titles than that. They are uncomfortable dealing with the common tactics negotiating. Procurement people know that and take advantage of it. If you are comfortable with it, then you have just wasted your money and your time. As for me, I get angry at first, and then I cool off and figure out what needs to be done so that I don't get victimized by the tactics that others are going to use against me. That's part of my job as I have defined it.

Here's a little secret: If you are a customer-facing individual and are responsible in some way, shape, or form for dealing with customers in a way that closes or extends business, sales, orders, or whatever you call it, your job is to do things that are in the best interest of your company.

It doesn't make any difference if you are a senior executive or a salesperson slogging it out in the trenches—if you are dealing with customers who are going to be buying from you, your job is to understand the game, understand the tactics that will be used to get you to do things that are not in the best interest of your company, and employ tactics that get the best things (profitable business) for your company.

Negotiating with backbone means being a cool and logical professional. I'm not that good at being cool and logical, but I can do it if I think about it. That's what being a professional is. Professionals aren't supposed to get angry, but I get angry. I try to use that anger to motivate me to think about the situation, decide on what the right tactics are, take notes on what those tactics are (doing my homework!), and use those tactics after I've cooled down. There is an important point here. I've written the darn book, and I still have to think about and practice what I am preaching. So don't expect that for you any of my suggestions are going to be easy.

If you need emotion to motivate you to do the right thing, then use it. If you need to get angry at the tactics being used against you, then get angry. Don't feel bad. Don't feel that you are not worthy. Get angry, get off your butt, and start thinking about the things you need to do to not be victimized by the tactics that a procurement person (or any manager, for that matter) is using against you. Then cool off, take your notes, delay if you have to in order to cool down, and then coolly execute the plan that you put together.

Never stoop to the level that they want you to. Never get angry with them or stoop to name calling. Never say something that will be used against you and that you will regret. That's not professional behavior. Don't be afraid to call out the tactic, though. If a client tries to use good cop/bad cop against you (refer to Chapter 2, "The Tells of the Game), call out the tactic, compliment him on trying to use it, and ask to meet with the bad cop. If you do, and can meet with the bad cop, she will try to rip you up one side and down the other. Let her do it. Sit and take it. Take lots of good notes on what she says to you. When she stops, ask whether she is finished. By the way, just by doing the two preceding things, you will rattle the good cop/bad cop team. They are expecting you to get rattled, but frankly, I like to rattle back. When they are finished, review the things they have said to you, and then ask them whether they are true. Point out that you know that your product is not a commodity because you have been a valued supplier to their organization for the past five years. Tell them that if they want a discount then you are perfectly willing to give them a discount but it will require taking some services away, delays in shipping, or providing products that don't have the features they have requested. Call them out and play the game better than they do—that's what professionals do.

Develop your plan and stick to it. In your notes you should have comments from your clients and others about criteria for selection, your history, and a competitor's value drivers and history. In the negotiation discussion revisit some of those prior quotes. Ask clients to identify what has changed about the situation. Ask them which of the prior comments was not true and indicate your willingness to go back to those individuals to find out what's going on.

At that point, the procurement person will do one of two things. The aggressive ones will try to up their game to rattle you. They'll tell you that they are in charge of the negotiations now and you are no longer permitted to talk to the decision makers with whom you've spent so much time cultivating relationships. These procurement people need to have absolute control. My recommended response: Call their bluff and walk out. Remember why you are there in the first place: You have value, and they recognize you have value. That's what makes you the Advantaged Player. They have made an investment in you, so leverage that value, be a professional, and get up and leave before they do. Tell them that you have been pleased with their business in the past and hope to establish it again in the future, but they are trying to push you to a point where you are no longer be able to serve them at a reasonable profit. Then get up and walk out. Make them sweat for a bit. Show some confidence.

The only one thing that could cause you to question the wisdom of walking away is that you have misdiagnosed the situation. If you're worried about that, the only thing to do is go back, review your basic assumptions, determine your scenario, and review the tactics appropriate for the scenario. Remember the bottom line: If you have no relationship with the decision maker, then you shouldn't be at the negotiation. If you have the relationship and provide the value, the tactics are appropriate and effective.

For me, William F. Buckley, the great conservative publisher of the *National Review*, demonstrated the kind of backbone I'm trying to encourage in this book. He was also an expert price negotiator. Let me share two stories about Buckley's expression of confidence in negotiations. One was from the very beginning of his career; the other toward the end.

In the mid-1960s, William F. Buckley was just starting his career as a lecturer. He was invited to speak at the University of Texas. The *Daily Texan* university newspaper was rather liberal at the time and criticized the university for paying Buckley a speaker's fee that was apparently larger than any fee received by previous speaker. A furious front-page editorial questioned whether the young speaker was worth it. Buckley spoke at the basketball auditorium. The bleachers and floor were packed with students, and excitement was in the air. How would Buckley react to the criticism about his fee? Buckley had a copy of the *Daily Texan* in his hand as he walked out to the podium. He held the paper up for all to see, and in his stentorian voice read the most accusatory part of the article aloud. He then turned to the audience and said, "I never said I was worth it. I only said I wouldn't do it for less." The audience erupted in rollicking applause that lasted more than a minute.

The second story concerns a letter to the editor sent to the *National Review* by a subscriber who took umbrage at one of Buckley's editorials. After explaining why he thought the editorial in question was the stupidest thing he ever read, the subscriber wrote, "And cancel my subscription!" Buckley published the letter in its entirety. In his response, he wrote only this: "Cancel your own goddamn subscription!" Buckley isn't a victim. He's proud of who he is and what he does. He has plenty of backbone.

An interesting question is whether the strategy of selling high value products and services is dead. I don't believe it is. It hasn't worked in many situations despite massive resources being poured into doing things better for clients. It hasn't worked not because customers don't value what suppliers do for them. They still do and they always will. The problem is that high value gets gutted on the negotiation table, and the investment that salespeople pursue with idealistic confidence gets discounted away in the desperation pricing that procurement people so much like to take advantage of.

To be successful in doing good things for customers, salespeople have to realistically pursue negotiations tactics that will not come naturally to them. (Well, these tactics might come naturally to some people, but it certainly didn't come naturally to me.) It comes from a clear understanding that salespeople are deserving of the prices we charge because of the value we provide to our customers.

You might argue that these approaches won't work in every situation. If so, at least it is closer to the truth of what is happening in the field of selling and negotiating today. They have worked in every case that I have every used or advised it to be used. The tactics provide solutions to the problems with the current selling and negotiating systems and provide a clear path for salespeople and managers to do the best things possible for their firms, which benefits everyone.

In the end, it takes backbone. Backbone comes from the knowledge that our job is to do the right things for both ourselves and our firms. Backbone requires an understanding of the situation we are in.

It takes an understanding of the tactics customers will use against us. Moreover, it takes a good understanding of the things we need to do to appropriately respond to those tactics. It comes from the knowledge that what we are doing is and will be supported by the leaders and managers in our firm. So go forward, better armed to negotiate in the great game of procurement, with knowledge, better skills, and certainly with backbone.

Index

O-P